CONTEND

Defending the Faith in a Fallen World

Aaron Armstrong
Cruciform Press | October, 2012

For Andrew, Chris, Noel, and Norm, pastors who
model contending for the faith to the glory of God —
and for Emily, who pushes me to do likewise.
- Aaron Armstrong

CruciformPress

"*Contend*, by one of evangelicalism's most promising young writers and thinkers, is exactly the kind of book the church needs in our moment. We are tempted today on every side to be meek as a mouse. Christianity is many things, but it is not—it cannot be—anodyne. Armstrong's gospel-saturated writing, coupled with deeply instructive practical examples, will equip the church to be as bold as a lion, and to roar as Luther, Calvin, Spurgeon, and Machen before us."

Owen Strachan, Assistant Professor of Christian Theology and Church History, Boyce College; coauthor, *Essential Edwards Collection*

"At a time of great theological confusion and emotional calls to content-less 'unity,' a time of politically-correct 'can't-we-all-get-alongism,' here is a balanced and passionate appeal especially to young believers from a young author, Aaron Armstrong, to take seriously their commitment to Jesus in all areas of life, both individually and in community, contending for the Faith, using both their minds and their hearts in defense of the Truth, in the manner laid out by the apostle Jude. May this call be heard far and wide."

Dr. Peter Jones, Executive Director, truthXchange, Scholar-in-Residence and Adjunct Professor, Westminster Seminary in California

"*Contend* is a fine combination of concise biblical exposition, down-to-earth examples, contemporary illustrations, and challenging practical application. I've already made a list of people I want to give this to…as well as another list of areas to work on in my own life and ministry. It's not only an ideal book for discipling a new believer, but also for shaking the more mature out of dangerous complacency and passivity."

Dr. David P. Murray, Professor of Old Testament and Practical Theology, Puritan Reformed Theological Seminary

"Some church leaders like myself get a queasy stomach when faced with theological conflicts. Others relish the fights and want to convene a church council over the number of Adam's hairs. Aaron presents a third way between avoidance and division: the biblical model of earnest, charitable contending for the faith. This is a book the Church desperately needs, for it matters not merely that we contend, but also how we contend and that we contend for the right cause: namely the name of Christ. *Contend* not only calls us to defend orthodoxy, but gives us a biblical blueprint for doing it. I wholeheartedly recommend this book to pastors, seminarians, bloggers, and teachers."

Daniel Darling, Senior Pastor, Gages Lake Bible Church; Author, *Real: Owning Your Christian Faith*

"The very idea of contending is contentious. But the costs of not contending for the faith are high, and we'd better learn when and how to defend what matters most. With clarity and insight, Aaron Armstrong helps us understand why it's hard to take a stand, what's worth fighting for, and how to do it. I'm grateful for this biblical and helpful book."

Darryl Dash, Pastor, Liberty Grace Church, Toronto ON; blogger, Dashhouse.com

"While some think that defending the faith is the task of scholarship and others dismiss it as the practice of rigid guardians of doctrine, my friend Aaron Armstrong reminds us that Jude's instruction is the Christian's necessity for perseverance in the faith, the advance of the gospel, and the glory of Christ. Filled with humble boldness and delight in the gospel, *Contend* will equip you with a biblical framework and practical advice to winsomely and wisely stand as a witness for Christ."

Andrew Hall, Lead Pastor, Community Bible Church, Ilderton ON

CruciformPress
something new in Christian publishing

Our Books: Clear. Direct. Inspiring. Gospel-focused. About 100 pages. *Print; 3 ebook formats.*

Consistent Prices: Every book costs the same.

Subscription Options: Print books or ebooks delivered to you on a set schedule, at a discount. Or buy print books or ebooks individually.

Pre-paid or Recurring Subscriptions
Print Book (list $9.99)................$6.49 each
Ebook (list $7.50)....................$3.99 each

Non-Subscription Sales
1-5 Print Books......................$8.45 each
6-50 Print Books.....................$7.45 each
More than 50 Print Books.............$6.45 each
Single Ebooks (bit.ly/CPebks).........$5.45 each
Bundles of 7 Ebooks...................$35.00
Ebook Distribution Program......6 pricing levels

Contend: Defending the Faith in a Fallen World

Print / PDF ISBN:	978-1-936760-60-2
ePub ISBN:	978-1-936760-62-6
Mobipocket ISBN:	978-1-936760-61-9

Table of Contents

Chapters

One
THE CONTEXT

Contending in Our Day

"To struggle in the face of opposition."

"To strive against rivals."

"To dispute and debate earnestly."

Contend is not a passive word, as these phrases from various dictionary definitions make clear. Contending requires action. And while it may sound like something polite people simply don't do, the fact is that we all contend. Asserting our opinions, vocalizing our likes and dislikes, broadcasting our beliefs, defending our positions—whether our point is profound or trivial, most of us go through the day fully primed to pass along our views to others.

Not on everything, obviously. But each of us will contend over those things that really matter to us. That's how you know what people care about.

Die-hard sports fans contend over the merits of their respective teams. People of differing political persuasions contend over parties and pragmatism, policies, and power. Companies contend with their rivals. Parents contend against whatever they think is harmful to their children. Nations contend with one another when they perceive a threat. When something that really matters to you is in harm's way, that's when you will be willing to contend — to struggle and strive, dispute and debate, even if it's uncomfortable.

The New Testament writer Jude (the brother of James and half-brother of our Lord) made an important point about this kind of principled striving when he wrote, "Beloved, although I was very eager to write to you about our common salvation, I found it necessary to write appealing to you to contend for the faith that was once for all delivered to the saints."[1]

One thing we can draw from Jude's appeal is that sometimes it is more important to defend the faith than to examine and rehearse what we believe. Like the writer of Ecclesiastes, Jude is affirming that there is a time and purpose for all godly behavior. To face inward, affirming and clarifying among and between orthodox believers everything God has done for us — this is a necessary, ongoing activity of the church. But that must not and cannot be our exclusive preoccupation. We must also at times — as a necessary complementary activity — be intentional about facing outward, contending with those who deny who God is and what he has done, whether these voices come from within the church or without.

Because sin and evil are ever at work, and their principal objective is to overthrow the gospel of grace, it's safe to say there has never been a time in the history of the church when contending was not necessary. Therefore, as if there were any doubt, this is certainly such a time.

Where We Are and How We Got Here

The Christian church in the West has come to a strange place. Many of us are so concerned about being perceived as judgmental or exclusive that we present to the world a false picture of "the faith that was once for all delivered to the saints." Indeed, a whole generation of young people (both Christian and not) are focused on unity[2] a to a degree that is not good for the church or the world. It's not that Christians with a strong interest in unity have wicked motives. We all want people to like us—and by extension to like Jesus. But when we place too high a priority on unity, we fail to contend for the faith.

How Millennials Think

Thom and Jess Rainer have published some helpful research on the Millennials, sometimes called Generation Y or Mosaics. Born between about 1980 and 2000, this generation, while less monolithic than some previous generations, does have some clear tendencies. Paradoxically, they "tend to be upbeat, positive, and happy. But they are realists as well."[3] They place more focus on family (sometimes quite loosely defined) than their Boomer and Gen X predecessors, yet few Millennials give thought to religious matters, and they generally see ethnic, racial, and sexual diversity as nonissues. Mixed-ethnic marriages, which would have ruffled feathers in previous generations, are normal for this generation, and even same-sex marriage is fine in the eyes of many.[4] Millennials have had enough of social division and believe it's their responsibility to pursue societal harmony as an end in itself:

9

Millennials are weary of the fights in our nation and world. They are tired of the polarization of views. They avoid the high-pitched shouts of opposing political forces. They are abandoning churches in great numbers because they see religion as divisive and argumentative.[5]

This, the Rainers suggest, may be this generation's defining issue. The Millennials, especially the Christian cohort, grew up seeing their parents locked into "culture wars" that divided people over music and dress codes, food and drink, festivals and feasts.[6] Frustrated by the seemingly endless quarrelling, they have declared their elders' contending as nothing more than "vanity, and a striving after the wind."[7] Having concluded that their parents' efforts in these areas were ultimately futile, they now want nothing of it. They want to know why we can't all just get along, explain the Rainers.[8]

I'm not pinning exclusive blame on the Millennials (among whom, by some definitions, I would be counted). Their desire for everyone to "just get along" is understandable and, as we see in Jude's letter, it goes back to the earliest days of the church.

Doctrine or unity? The community of believers to whom Jude wrote his epistle had been infiltrated by false teachers intent on deception. These teachers were actively trying to turn the eyes of the Christian community away from Christ. Yet, instead of rejecting these apostles of Satan and their demonic doctrine,[9] the believers accepted them. Perhaps it was out of simple naïveté or maybe theological ignorance, but whatever the reason, the Christians to whom Jude appealed did not recognize these teachers for the "fierce wolves" they truly were.

The experience of Jude's audience is far from unique. Christians in every age have suffered the attacks of false teachers. In the New Testament alone,

- Paul faced Judaizers and "super-apostles" who insisted that keeping the ceremonial law was necessary for our justification.[10]
- The apostle John seemingly squared off against mystics who were more concerned with esoteric knowledge than the truth of the gospel.[11]
- In his revelation to John, Jesus himself rebuked the Nicolaitans who sought to spread sexual immorality throughout the church at Ephesus and Pergamum.[12]

Since those days, the Church has repeatedly needed to be drawn back to Scripture and away from the lure of false teaching. Here are just a few more examples:

- Numerous battles were waged against various heresies in the first few centuries of the church.
- Augustine defended the doctrine of original sin against Pelagius in the fourth century.
- Luther, Calvin, and the Reformers upheld biblical authority over against the Roman Church in the sixteenth century.
- Evangelical stalwarts J. I. Packer, Francis Schaeffer, and J. Gresham Machen contended against the creep

of liberalism and easy-believism in the early- and mid-twentieth centuries.

In each of these cases, the counterattacks mounted by Christians were successful, in the sense that many believers were awakened to the danger of false teaching and renewed their commitment to sound doctrine. Inevitably, though, the Church's fresh zeal would, over time, cool into passivity before slipping finally into apostasy—typically within the relatively short span of three or four generations. Where one generation believed the truth, the second assumed it and the third denied it, as D. A. Carson frequently reminds us.[13] But in every instance, when truth is denied by one generation, God mercifully brings about a renewal in the next.

<u>False teaching today.</u> Our own day is indeed desperate for renewal. In recent years, virtually no fundamental belief of the Christian faith has been free from assault, even from professing believers. The virgin birth, the inspiration and authority of Scripture, the sinlessness of Christ, even the necessity of the physical resurrection: everything seems open for debate.[14]

How did things get this bad? It boggles the mind, especially when we consider the sheer volume of solid, Christ-exalting books and sermons available in our time. Still, here we are. While there are undoubtedly many reasons for this sad development (and what follows is not at all a comprehensive analysis), I would like to try to tie together a few related threads:

Thread 1: Millennials are especially inclined to the pursuit of (perceived) unity.

Thread 2: The mainstream cultural air we breathe — celebrating tolerance and political correctness — pressures us all, regardless of age, to embrace (perceived) unity as the highest good.

Thread 3: Many Millennial Christians have been exposed to the weaknesses of seeker-sensitive churches and modern fundamentalism (we will review these influences in a moment).

Thread 4: Responding or reacting to these various influences, many millennials fled to various expressions of the emerging/emergent church.

Tie these threads together, and you get a tangled, messy knot characterized by a de-emphasis of doctrine leading to a largely rudderless unity-for-its-own-sake kind of unity.

But I'm getting ahead of myself. Let's go back and look at what the unity-loving millennials have grown up with in Western evangelicalism.

What Millennials Have Seen

The Seeker-Sensitive Movement. Birthed out of a genuine desire to see the lost come to a saving faith in Jesus Christ, the seeker-sensitive movement[15] sought to eliminate as many perceived barriers to faith as possible. In their view, perhaps the most challenging barrier facing the non-Christian was an emphasis on doctrine. Doctrine divides, or so the saying goes. So, rather than offering non-Christians doctrine-heavy expository preaching, it was thought better to attend to their felt needs with shorter, topical messages, dramatic presentations, and heart-warming music.

And it worked. Sort of.

Lots of people came through the doors of seeker-sensitive churches. Lots of people made professions of faith and began participating in church activities. But as time went on, it came as a rude surprise that these people weren't necessarily growing in their faith.

"We discovered that higher levels of church activity did not predict increasing love for God or increasing love for other people," writes Cally Parkinson in Willow Creek's Reveal study.[16] People weren't growing, nor were they taking ownership of their spiritual growth.[17] Simply put, the seeker-sensitive model seemed to do a fine job of making converts but a poor job of making disciples. "Our analysis paints the picture of the church being too preoccupied with the early growing years, leaving the spiritual adolescents to find their own way—without preparing them for the journey."[18]

I'm not making a categorical statement that all seeker churches neglect discipleship, nor am I saying that God cannot work through these methods to accomplish his will. Indeed, my wife and I came to genuine faith at such a church.

Looking back, however, it's clear we were not discipled. We survived—and before long moved on to another congregation—because God was motivating my growth in ways that the leaders were not. Indeed, given the materials I was reading and listening to in my earliest days as a believer, it's a wonder I wasn't shipwrecked right from the start.

This discipleship issue—the failure to prepare the "spiritual adolescents" for the journey—is at the heart of the Church's current predicament over contending for the faith. And there are a lot of those adolescents in American churches. Willow Creek (Bill Hybels), Saddleback (Rick Warren), North Point Community Church (Andy Stanley), Elevation Church (Steven Furtick), Newspring Church (Perry Noble), Lakewood Church (Joel Osteen), and Oak Hills Church (Max Lucado) see a combined 144,000 people come through their doors every single week.[19] Add in sermon downloads, books, blogs, conference appearances, etc., and the numbers rise far higher. The influence of seeker methodology is enormous, with hundreds of thousands in North America alone directly influenced by it on a regular basis.

Of course, a primary focus of these churches is simply to get people in the door, and many of them enjoy remarkable success. As a result, a great many people in the West who began calling themselves Christians not too many years ago are now active in local churches without having had the benefit of much sound, expository preaching or effective discipleship.

To put it another way, a large chunk of an entire generation of believers has been largely left to its own devices to figure out the Christian faith.

Modern Fundamentalism. But the seeker-sensitive movement is not the only force that has weakened Christian doctrine and practice in our day. Fundamentalism, in the modern, sectarian sense of the term, is equally responsible. Where seeker churches are geared toward having a good experience and sometimes shave off the hard edges of the gospel in the process, <u>fundamentalists have replaced the gospel with moralism,</u> piling a burden upon the men and women in their congregations that is more than anyone could bear. Listening to the music of Amy Grant, reading any translation other than the King James, missing the Sunday evening service, even being happy at church meetings — in some places any of these may be interpreted as signs that you're out of the kingdom. Where the seeker movement frequently produces believers who lack a foundation in the gospel, fundamentalism often produces believers who lack any assurance of the gospel.

The Backlash

The late 1990s and early 2000s saw evangelicalism abuzz over this thing called "the emerging church."[20] No one was quite sure what it was, but they were excited about it. Weary of what they perceived as a lack of authenticity in the seeker movement and turned off by the loveless, wrathful God of fundamentalism, youngish pastors and leaders began looking for a way to reconnect Christianity with real life. They wanted a place where it was "okay to not be okay," a place where doubts could be voiced freely, where questions could be asked without fear of negative consequences, and where authentic faith could come alive.

But in their commitment to asking questions and expressing doubt — things we should never have a problem with — some forgot that there still had to be a foundation, a standard of truth. So while some questioned the way to "do church," and some asked about how best to communicate the core truths of Christianity, others began to question the necessity or even the validity of basic Christian doctrines.

Did Jesus really have to be born of a virgin? Is the Bible really the inspired Word of God or is it merely a collection of folklore representing a nomadic people's evolving understanding of God? Is the idea of hell consistent with a God of love? One writer within this movement made an alarming observation: "The idea that there is a necessary distinction of matter from spirit, or creation from creator, is being reconsidered."[21]

When you don't understand that there are some things worth contending for, everything is up for grabs.

A Case Study in Backlash

Today, although the emerging movement has more or less run out of steam, its influence is still powerfully felt, particularly as pastors and authors within its revisionist stream (now often called the emergent church) continue to write books and blogs and, as in the case of Rob Bell, develop a television series as part of his goals to share "the message of God's love with a broader audience." Indeed, for many within evangelicalism, Bell is the first who comes to mind when they hear "emerging," though he has done his best to avoid such labels.

Raised in a traditional Christian home in Ingham County, Michigan, Bell studied at Wheaton College and Fuller Theological Seminary before moving to Grand Rapids to study under Ed Dobson, pastor of Calvary Chapel, where he and his wife began to consider what

planting a new kind of community would look like. In
1998, Bell planted Mars Hill Bible Church. In less than
three years, weekly attendance ranged from 2,000 to 3,500.
A few more years, and that number had ballooned to
between 8,000 and 11,000 per week. Despite the church's
success, it wasn't long before Bell and his wife became
uncomfortable with church. "Life in the church had
become so small," Kristen Bell says. "It had worked for
me for a long time. Then it stopped working."[22] As writer
Andy Crouch observes:

> The Bells started questioning their assumptions about
> the Bible itself — "discovering the Bible as a human
> product," as Rob puts it, rather than the product of
> divine fiat. "The Bible is still in the center for us," Rob
> says, "but it's a different kind of center. We want to
> embrace mystery, rather than conquer it."[23]

Weary of the black-and-white world of evangelicalism and burnt out from trying to do life as a
"superpastor,"[24] Bell found comfort in Brian McLaren's
book *A New Kind of Christian*.[25] Chronicling the
fictional relationship between disillusioned evangelical
pastor Dan Poole and high school teacher/spiritual guide
Neo (himself a lapsed pastor), *A New Kind of Christian*
walks readers "through a series of set pieces that introduce
the initially skeptical Dan to a 'postmodern' approach
to Christianity"[26] — one that shuns the divisive nature of
absolutes, the clear-cut categories of evangelicalism. It's no
surprise, then, that in Bell's writing, as in many among this

revisionist set, even the notion of contending is anathema. We see this in Bell's derisive and ill-conceived discussion of what he calls "brickianity" where (among other things),

> You spend a lot of time talking about how right you are. Which of course leads to how wrong everybody else is. Which then leads to defending the wall.... [but] you rarely defend a trampoline. You invite people to jump on it with you.[27]

Presumably, Bell views most traditional Christianity as consumed with "defending the wall" (hence, "brickianity") when he would rather jump on trampolines. This analogy is troubling for many reasons, not the least of which being that even a trampoline requires a sturdy frame to keep it together. The complaint that "brickianity" is all about defending the wall for the sake of defending the wall is worth considering, but that does not mean that no one should ever contend for the faith. Imagine I said to my wife, "Emily, I love you so much that I shouldn't have to defend you when someone speaks ill of you. You're cool with that, right?" What about if I said that to my children? How do you think that would go for me?

This idea that we don't need to defend—or at best rarely need to defend—something we love is ludicrous. If we are willing to offer defense for our families, our political preferences, and the Toronto Maple Leafs, how much more should we be willing to offer a defense of the gospel? If we truly love Jesus and if we truly care about the well being of the Church then we must contend.

Contending Defined

Let's be honest: doctrine sometimes does divide. It can't not by its very nature. Jesus himself—the Word of God made flesh—was and is the most divisive person ever to live. He himself said, "Do you think that I have come to give peace on earth? No, I tell you, but rather division."[28]

The ultimate question about Jesus today is the same as when he walked the earth: is he or is he not who he claimed to be? He said, "I am the way, and the truth, and the life. No one comes to the Father except through me."[29] With the entire Christian faith standing or falling on the validity of such an utterly exclusive and uncompromising claim, doctrine that truly aligns with Jesus will cause division. When we discuss our faith honestly, it is simply inevitable: at times we will be at odds with others— friends, relatives, perhaps even other believers.

Yet we are called to contend—in obedience to and for the sake of the most divisive person in history. And the challenge is to do it in the way Jude describes. We'll unpack this more in the following chapters, but our premise, and a key takeaway for this entire book, is simply this:

Contending must be understood and exercised as an act of mercy toward those who doubt and those who have been deceived, regardless of whether they claim faith in Christ.

The question we must now answer is, "Over what must we contend?" That's the focus of the next chapter.

Two
THE CONTENT

Contending for God and for the Gospel

Like all married couples, my wife and I occasionally express our disagreements with a certain unhelpful zeal … okay, we fight. But, however important the issue might seem at the time, we have come to realize that our disputes are often over stupid or trivial things:

- Was there an episode of the *Ewoks* cartoon with Storm Troopers?[30]
- In answer to the question, "What time is it?" is there a meaningful difference between "A little after three" and "3:07"?
- If I go into another room to get something for my wife, is this actually helpful to her if she didn't ask for my help?

These are the kinds of deep, confounding issues that can arise in a marriage, right? No, these are the kinds of ultimately insignificant questions that we find ourselves squabbling over mainly so we can claim the title of Rightest Person in the Room.

Sometimes this is what modern evangelicalism can look like, too. Depending on the books you read, the conferences you attend, and the blogs you visit, in recent years you may have watched as untold hours were spent analyzing and articulating every detail and nuance of a range of secondary issues.

- What is the best church model?
- What is the ideal level of contextualization (adjusting how you talk about the gospel for the sake of a particular audience)?
- What is the right way to educate our kids (public, Christian, charter, or homeschooling)?

I'm not saying these issues, and a dozen others like them, do not matter, but when is too much just too much? All this time and energy? Invested by all these people? Really? What's worse, at some point the debate itself becomes the focus. What's actually on the table is no longer, say, church government, but who is Righter than whom.

All this intensity over a raft of secondary issues. Meanwhile, essential issues often fail to get the attention they deserve from professing believers. And a sea of churchgoers—namely, the Millenials—shake their heads and start looking for other paths.

How do we know the difference between primary and secondary issues? And how does knowing help us in our duty to contend? The best place to start is by defining what's primary.

There are a handful of doctrines upon which the Church stands or falls. These do not shift to maintain alignment with social trends, nor are they difficult to identify—they have been articulated and defended throughout church history. The early church fathers summarized them in their creeds, notably the Apostles' and Nicene Creeds, which are still widely used today. The Reformers did so again in the five *solas* and later expounded upon them in great detail in the Heidelberg and Westminster catechisms. In the late 19th and early 20th centuries, R. A. Torrey and a number of other Bible teachers once more formulated what they believed to be the essentials of the Christian faith and published them in the 12-volume series *The Fundamentals*. What we find as we examine the work of the fathers, the Reformers, and contemporary theologians is that they keep returning to three particular themes:

- The authority of Scripture
- God's nature and character
- The gospel

We will get to the authority of Scripture later, after we consider God and the gospel.

We Contend for the Doctrine of God

There was a time when if you used the term "God," nearly everyone would know you were referring to the God of the Bible. Today, "God" could mean almost anything—

from the triune God of Christianity to the god of any of several other religions to a vague cosmic force to the earth itself. The existence of a personal God who can be known by individuals — the God revealed in the Bible — is no longer assumed in our spiritual-but-nonreligious world. If we are to truly contend for the faith, holding fast to the truth of the gospel and the inspiration of Scripture, this is where we must begin. We must begin with God.

Imagine you're standing dominoes up in a line to watch them fall. You've set up all your pieces just so and you're ready to push the lead one. If you've got that first domino in the right place, when you knock it down, the chain reaction can begin, with every properly situated piece falling in exactly the right way. But if your first domino is pointing in the wrong direction or is placed too far away from the others, it's just not going to work.

Our understanding of God is kind of like that. <u>If we get God wrong, nothing else will truly fall in place.</u> We won't understand the gospel and there will be no energy or momentum to drive us forward into a life of fruitful labor to the glory of God. Thankfully, due to the immeasurable gift of the Bible, we have everything we need to get that first "domino" right.[31] Indeed, if we begin to grasp even the most basic truths regarding God's nature and character, that changes everything.

God's Nature: Immanent, Transcendent, Triune

We find a tremendous statement about God's nature in the psalmist's joyful proclamation, "O Lord, our Lord, how majestic is your name in all the earth! You have set your glory above the heavens."[32] In theological terms, the first sentence in that verse refers to God's *immanence* and the second refers to his *transcendence*.

Immanent. There is a lot packed into, "how majestic is your name in all the earth." Here on *earth*, a *name* (used by David in the sense of reputation and renown) describes who someone really is at the core. This majestic God has partially revealed himself to us—he has a name, and that means that we can comprehend him, at least to some degree. God's self-revelation brings him near and makes him personal.

Indeed, God is intimately involved in his creation, and particularly so by making mankind in his image. Not content to speak the first man and woman into being, God actually formed them with his hands.[33] Apparently there is a sense in which this direct formation continues, for the psalmist declares that God "formed my inward parts; [he] knitted me together in my mother's womb."[34] It seems only fitting that a sovereign, loving God would play a "hands-on" role in the formation of every creature specifically made in his image.

God's moment-by-moment involvement with us does not end at birth, though, continuing throughout our lives. Jesus goes so far as to tell us that God "knows what you need before you ask him."[35] Indeed, Jesus himself is the epitome of the immanence of God—humbling himself to take on flesh, becoming like us so that he might redeem us. This is not the description of a far-off, unknowable, uninterested divine being. It is instead a realistic, if partial, glimpse of a deeply personal, involved God.

God is *immanent*; he is near and knowable.

Transcendent. Even as God delights to make himself known to us, we can only know him in part; the fullness of God's glory is at this time far beyond our perception or ability to comprehend. On earth, what we know of God is truly majestic, but his glory extends beyond the heavens — beyond all we can see and all we can imagine. When we say that God is *transcendent*, we do not deny his immanence; rather, we say that *in addition*, he is infinitely above and beyond his creation. He is not a part of the world in the way that we are, and it is not a part of him.

While God is infinite in all his attributes, one particular way the Bible underscores this is by emphasizing that God is *eternal.* The Bible never shows us the Creator's starting point, for he has none. Instead, it begins with *the starting point of creation.* In the beginning, before the foundations of the world were laid, God was.[36] There has never been a time when God was not. He "was and is and is to come … the Alpha and the Omega, the beginning and the end."[37] This is our transcendent God.

Consider for a moment the implications of misperceiving or denying that God is either transcendent or immanent.

A supreme being who is not transcendent? Such a being would not be God at all. He would need the universe for his existence — either because he is part of the universe or because he depends upon the universe in the same way we depend upon the earth for our physical lives.

Such a god would simply be another player jostling for power in a giant struggle in the heavens.

Hinduism, Buddhism, Sufism, and the New Spirituality movement (promoted by Oprah, Eckhart Tolle, Marianne Williamson, Rhonda Byrne, and many others) are among those who ultimately deny the transcendence of God as revealed in Scripture. In their view, all is one. God, whether manifesting as a person, a cosmic force, or in the divine self, is just one more part of the eternal cosmos.

A supreme being who is not immanent? At best, such a god would be uninvolved with mankind in any sort of caring, relational way, and at worst would be completely unknowable and unapproachable.

- If such a god communicated his wishes to mankind, you *might* try to live by them. More likely, though, seeing his rules as arbitrary standards not grounded in love for you, you would live in constant fear that you could not live up to those standards, so you would spend your life in futile rebellion or in frantic acts of legalistic, performance-based paranoia.
- If such a God did *not* communicate his wishes to mankind, then you would find yourself in an even worse situation, adrift in a meaningless, clueless existence.

Islam and Christian-like cults such as the Jehovah's Witnesses, Mormons, and the Seventh-day Adventists do not believe in an immanent God. We know this particu-

larly because of their view of salvation: none of these
groups believes in a God who draws near to truly and
completely save his people. While each claims divine revelation, their views of God, man, and salvation are bleak.
Each believes that:

> ### Faith (in Christ or, in Islam's case, Allah)
> ### + Good Works
> ### = Salvation

Christianity, however, teaches that:

> ### Faith in Christ =
> ### Salvation + Good Works

No other religion or worldview offers this good
news. They always get the equation mixed up. But to get
the equation wrong is to get everything else wrong, too.
When good works are performed not out of gratitude but
to earn favor, then salvation becomes dependent on your
performance, not God's grace and mercy.

The religions that teach such damnable error can
appeal to us—and so can the gods they worship—because
they put us in the driver's seat, offering the illusion that we
are in control. While this appeals to our fallen nature, it
is nothing more than a repackaging of exactly what Paul
condemns: "they exchanged the truth about God for a
lie and worshiped and served the creature rather than the
Creator."[38] These "gods" are plainly made in our own
image and likeness. They are easily controlled, easily

manipulated, and, ultimately, easily ignored. They have no authority. They have no power. Although possessing an ability to deceive that can be tragic for mankind, compared to the God who is, they ultimately don't matter.

Triune. The twin truths of God's immanence and transcendence come together in the doctrine of the Trinity—the truth that our God is one in essence and three in persons who exist in eternal, perfect, joyful communion with one another.

- He is the eternal heavenly Father, the maker of heaven and earth, who ordains the redemption of the elect and sent forth Jesus to accomplish it.[39]
- He is Jesus, the only begotten Son of God; the Word who was with God and was God, the one by whom and for whom all things were made; the one Lord to whom the Father has given all glory, honor, and power; the one who accomplishes redemption for us in perfect obedience to the will of God.[40]
- He is the Holy Spirit, the Helper who applies Christ's righteousness, regenerating and renewing those who were slaves to evil, sealing and sanctifying God's people for the day of redemption.[41]

God's Character: Above All, Holy

The God of the Bible—the triune, eternal, immanent/transcendent God who is the creator of all that was and is and ever will be—is the sovereign one, the supreme authority in the universe. No creature holds authority over him and "whatever the LORD pleases, he does."[42]

None can direct him or give him counsel,[43] nor can anyone say to him, "What have you done?"[44]

This picture of God should rightly cause us to tremble in abject fear—if that's all we know about him. But because God has revealed his character to us, we can rejoice! Why? Consider the ways the Bible speaks of God. He is love,[45] full of jealousy,[46] wrath,[47] and "mercy,"[48] but there is one characteristic that undergirds them all: holiness. "Holy, holy, holy is the LORD of hosts," the Seraphim sang in Isaiah's vision of the Lord, "the whole earth is full of his glory!"[49] God's holiness again calls to mind his being distinct from the world he has made, but more than that, "the word *holy* calls attention to all that God is," writes R. C. Sproul, "It reminds us that His love is holy love, His justice is holy justice, His mercy is holy mercy, His knowledge is holy knowledge, His spirit is holy spirit."[50]

The holiness of God reminds us that he is actually not "a petty, unjust, unforgiving control-freak; a vindictive, bloodthirsty ethnic cleanser; a misogynistic, homophobic, racist, infanticidal, genocidal, filicidal, pestilential, megalo-maniacal, sadomasochistic, capriciously malevolent bully"[51] like Richard Dawkins says he is. Nor is he, as Roger Olson suggests in his critique of Calvinist theology, a "moral monster" if he indeed rules and reigns to the degree that the Scriptures proclaim.[52] His holiness is instead a reminder that all he says and does—everything about him—is perfect, right and good, even when it's hard for us to understand.

1 Cor. 2:14

Thus, one absolute for which we must contend is the nature and character of God. The other absolute is the gospel.

We Contend for the Gospel

Paul provides the most succinct, accessible framework
for understanding the essential truth of the gospel: "For
I delivered to you as of first importance what I also
received: that Christ died for our sins in accordance with
the Scriptures, that he was buried, that he was raised on
the third day in accordance with the Scriptures."[53]

Notice Paul's insistence that without the death, burial,
and resurrection of Jesus, there is no gospel. Ephesians
1 spells out this truth in more detail, and John affirms it
when he writes, "In this is love, not that we have loved
God but that he loved us and sent his Son to be the propi-
tiation for our sins."[54]

The Bible uniformly depicts humanity in a desperate
condition, a hopelessness overcome only by the decisive
and merciful act of God the Father to send God the Son
into the world to live the life we could not live, to die in
our place, to rise again, and to give new life through God
the Spirit to those who believe. At every point, it is God
who acts, giving freely a priceless treasure to people who
could never earn it or deserve it.

The gospel is not about us. It is about God—God
who acts for his own infinitely deserving glory in ways
that redound to our infinite good.

But note also Paul's emphasis on the fact that Jesus'
death, burial, and resurrection, matters of the highest
possible importance, happened "in accordance with the
Scriptures." Paul is telling us that the primary purpose of
the Bible is to point to Christ and his gospel. Indeed, Jesus
himself rebuked the Pharisees because, in searching the

Scriptures for eternal life, they missed the fact that "it is they that bear witness about me."[55] Later, "beginning with Moses and all the Prophets, [Jesus] interpreted to [two of his disciples] in all the Scriptures the things concerning himself."[56]

Throughout the Bible, you can feel the presence of Jesus. He is there subtly in God's promise that the seed of the woman would crush the head of the serpent.[57] He is there powerfully in the promise of one on whom the Lord would lay all our iniquities.[58] Jude knew this, for he reminded his audience that it was "Jesus, who saved a people out of the land of Egypt,"[59] even though we do not read his name specifically in the Old Testament accounts of that great exodus. Jesus is the entire point of the gospel, and he is the entire point of Scripture. (Indeed, he is the entire point of human history and of creation—Alpha and Omega, the beginning and the end!)

Embracing the Truth to Encourage Others

Let's go back to the authority of Scripture. You may have noticed that the previous sections assume this essential truth[60] because if the Scripture is not the Word of God, then we cannot trust it as God's revelation of himself, nor can we know the nature and character of God or, indeed, the gospel itself. If we know God and the gospel, we know that the Scriptures are authoritative. They are a package deal—a kind of indivisible trinity of truth, a three-legged stool of mutual interdependence. We cannot, then, compromise on this reality or any of its elements.

We must hold fast to the truth of the Bible, not as a book of inspirational thoughts about God but as the record of his self-disclosure and of his plan to redeem his fallen creation through the gift of his Son.

Without these truths, we have no ground to contend for. We will be rudderless ships, left with only our opinions, incapable of showing the kind of mercy Jude pleads with us to show the doubting and deceived. But as we embrace these truths—not only accepting, but also rejoicing in them—we will be able to expose error with the light of Truth and encourage others to walk in that same light.

Three
THE CHALLENGE

Contending Well and Wisely

If contending for the faith is best seen as an act of mercy toward people who doubt or have been deceived, we must realize it is likely to get difficult and uncomfortable—emotionally messy. To contend for the faith is to force people (albeit in mercy) to confront the most important questions of human existence—questions like *Who am I? Who is God? Why am I here? What is all this about, anyway?* Contending, the way Jude uses the word, primarily involves doctrine—articulating what's true and what isn't. It therefore digs around in two areas that define who we are: contending digs around in peoples' *principles* and, to a lesser degree, in their *preferences*.

Principles are the foundational truths we hold to that undergird our beliefs, behaviors, and reasoning. Every one of us, Christian or not, makes judgment calls about good and bad, right and wrong, based on what we see as the sacred things—untouchable, unquestionable ideas of the highest importance.[61] Because our principles derive from our view of what's sacred, they define what we see as the primary, no-compromise issues.

• authority of Scripture
• God's character + nature
• the gospel

Preferences are the things we hold onto for a host
of reasons less profound than the sacred. Our preferences are manifested in the beliefs and practices we
embrace because we understand them, because they have
become traditions, because we think they produce good
for ourselves or others, or because they seem to follow
logically from our principles. But preferences are not
sacred, so we could, if absolutely necessary, let them go
without feeling like we were abandoning our very understanding of capital-T Truth.

You might think that Christians could all agree on the
principles, the really big issues that are primary and sacred.
After all, that's what Christianity is supposedly about—
some basic sacred tenets. But not all who profess faith in
Christ in our day would line up behind the issues set forth
as primary in the previous chapter: Scripture, God, and
the gospel. Indeed, many professing believers have serious
conflicts over what should be seen as primary. Consider
two broad categories of Christians whose principles
regularly collide.

Theological progressives. To make a rough general-
ization, theological progressives (or theological liberals[62])
in our day tend to see issues of *human rights* as sacred
and therefore primary. They want social progress and are
not especially concerned with whether the full counsel
of Scripture supports their views about what constitutes
social progress. Their motivations are frequently noble
and commendable, but they emphasize inclusiveness and
unity, and they are more likely to think of people as fundamentally good rather than as fundamentally fallen. This

presses their thinking in the direction of *man-centeredness*. Their mission is human freedom and flourishing, broadly defined.

Theological conservatives. Theological conservatives, on the other hand, tend to see as primary what they believe the Scripture says is primary. They (and I count myself among them) see the Bible as their controlling guide, and they are not especially concerned with whether sociological trends support their views. While respectful of various cultures and eras (because all people are made in God's image), they understand man basically as fallen rather than good. Because of this, they emphasize reconciliation between God and man as a prerequisite to true inclusiveness and unity. This presses their thinking toward *God-centeredness* and *Scripture-centeredness*. Their mission is the Great Commission.

To be sure, theological progressivism and theological conservatism are not opposed on every point. Human freedom and the Great Commission are hardly mortal enemies.[63] Moreover, in practice, individuals and groups can fall almost anywhere on the conservative–liberal spectrum. Therefore, we ought to be careful in making assumptions about a person's overall theological view based on a single issue, for few of us possess a theology that is wholly consistent on every point.

So we have principles and preferences, and we have the influences of our theological leanings. Now add in the fact that we are all unique individuals whose experiences, personality, and degree of maturity (not to mention a host of other factors) all influence whether we contend, why we contend, how we contend, what we contend about, and how we respond when drawn into contending conversation.

It's easy to see how things can get messy, isn't it? It's hard even to *think* clearly about all these factors, much less navigate our way through them when the time comes to transition from theory to practice.

But wait, there's more—there's also the fact that our world is being transformed by something that no other generation of Christians has faced. I refer, of course, to that Great Megaphone in the Cloud known as the Internet.

Biting and Devouring in Broadband

The Internet is essentially a massively complex technological expression of human nature. That's why it is so clearly both a good thing and a bad thing. All the wisdom and encouragement and insight of man can be promoted and, to a significant degree, communicated through the Internet. Likewise the foolishness, obsessions, petty grievances, and the tics and vices of humanity. So we have in one world wide web the bad stuff side-by-side with the good stuff, wheat and tares growing in the same field.

Indeed, the overriding characteristic of the Internet is its capacity to spread and amplify human expression with unprecedented speed and reach, with minimal burden on the user. On the web, very little is truly off limits. Billions of people can communicate whatever they want. And they do.

- Is there something that really bugs you? If you look hard enough, the Internet can endlessly fuel your indignation, join you in virtual camaraderie with others who share it, and provide you a platform for spreading it.
- Do you want to be seen as an expert? You can mine an infinite data stream online, so almost anyone can at least pretend to have attained wisdom.
- Do you crave some minor celebrity status? If you have the energy and the drive, all the tools you need to feed your selfish ambition are at your social-networking fingertips.

Again, since the web is an expression of human nature, and humans are dualistic creatures made in God's image yet horribly fallen, there *is* good on the web. Lots of it. We should never deny that. But when we sum up all that is *bad* about the web, we can do no better than the apostle James: "No human being can tame the tongue. It is a restless evil, full of deadly poison."[64]

James knows it is inevitable that if we communicate in words, our words will eventually spread evil. This connection cannot be broken. The web tempts us to talk, and our tongues want to start jabbering. As a result, more people talk to more people more frequently, more easily, about more things than ever before. And so sin abounds.[65] If James is right, more talk means there is more evil emerging than ever before—more, also, of evil's annoying little brother, foolishness.

Make no mistake: foolishness is a form of evil, for it

stands in opposition to God's wisdom and therefore in opposition to God. We might say, then, that one of the most common evils on the Internet is basic, old-school, garden-variety foolishness.

To judge from how Christians behave on the Internet, you'd think there are scores of primary, sacred issues worthy of all-out battle with fellow believers in public, complete with schoolyard taunts and the imputation of evil motives. Junior bloggers set themselves up as the theology police, thrashing those with whom they disagree and doing so with relative impunity or even the encouragement of readers who seem hungry for controversy. In their wake come the blog commenters, hiding behind aliases while firing off ill-considered rants, seemingly unaware of the damage such behavior can do both within the church and the world at-large. Think about unbelievers assessing the reputation of Christ by the online behavior of those who call themselves his disciples!

Such foolishness is not what Jude meant when he called us to contend for the faith. When believers "bite and devour one another"[66] in front of the entire world, we not only fail in our calling to contend, but we make it far easier for unbelievers to dismiss the gospel altogether.[67]

As many others have said, secondary issues are not unimportant—but they are truly *secondary*. This means, in part, that they do not stand alone, as if they are independent of the primary issues. Indeed, the secondary issues only have significance as they are tied to one or more primary issues—we only get to them by carefully and explicitly crossing the bridge of primary issues.[68]

This biblical approach serves everyone, Christian and non-Christian, by demonstrating that when rightly understood and presented, this faith to which we hold is coherent and internally consistent, with a definable set of core issues from which the secondary issues emerge.

Even then, believers may in good faith disagree on secondary issues without one party calling the other *an enemy of the gospel.* That phrase is reserved for false teaching with regard to primary issues. It is serious business, and the core focus of this book.

The Enemy Within

Take a moment and think of someone alive today whom you would consider an enemy of the gospel.

Do you have somebody in mind? Maybe it's someone like the strident atheist Richard Dawkins or new-age guru Deepak Chopra or Buddhist leader the Dalai Lama. These people have made their disagreement with Christianity plain, openly opposing the biblical gospel on its own terms, and they require a response in the form of apologetics, or reasonable defenses of the faith. Indeed, apologetics can certainly be understood as a form of contending, but the writers of Scripture do not primarily warn us about opponents like this — people outside of the church whose arguments against the faith require reasoned defense. Instead, Scripture consistently warns us that the most severe threats to the gospel come from within the church.

Jude's warning, let us remember, is that "certain people have *crept in* [to the church] *unnoticed.*"[69] His emphasis is not on those outside. His concern is far less with pagan priests than with those claiming the name of Jesus. Jude is not alone in this concern:

- Jesus warns, "Beware of false prophets, who come to you in sheep's clothing but inwardly are ravenous wolves."[70]
- Paul warned the Ephesian elders that "fierce wolves" would rise up from among their own number.[71]
- To the Corinthians, Paul said, "such men are false apostles, deceitful workmen, disguising themselves as apostles of Christ. And no wonder, for even Satan disguises himself as an angel of light. So it is no surprise if his servants, also, disguise themselves as servants of righteousness"[72]
- To the Philippians: "Look out for the dogs, look out for the evildoers, look out for those who mutilate the flesh."[73]
- To the Colossians: "Let no one disqualify you, insisting on asceticism and worship of angels, going on in detail about visions, puffed up without reason by his sensuous mind, and not holding fast to the Head."[74]
- To Timothy: "Certain persons, by swerving from these, have wandered away into vain discussion, desiring to be teachers of the law, without understanding either what they are saying or the things about which they make confident assertions."[75]
- Peter likewise warned "there will be false teachers among you, who will secretly bring in destructive heresies, even denying the Master who bought them."[76]

- John warned: "For many deceivers have gone out into the world, those who do not confess the coming of Jesus Christ in the flesh. Such a one is the deceiver and the antichrist."[77]

But perhaps the most terrifying warning is one Paul applies to himself, "But even if *we* or an angel from heaven.... If *anyone* is preaching to you a gospel contrary to the one you received, let him be accursed."[78] If Paul could look at himself and say, "If I start preaching a false gospel, may I go to hell," that should be motivation enough to approach false teaching with dread earnestness. We overlook the severity of these warnings to our peril.

False teachers don't usually make themselves obvious; they rarely look like Dick Dastardly with his sinister moustache, nor do they lurk in the bushes waiting to snatch you and tie you to the train tracks. Jude refers to them as "hidden reefs"[79] because they are often inconspicuous—at least, right up until the moment their teaching and way of life shipwreck you.

These people call themselves Christians but reject the truth. They are pastors of the serpent who say nice things and tickle our ears with words that make us feel good but actually deny Scripture—sometimes overtly, sometimes covertly. They effectively reject God's authority. Like Korah, they are in constant rebellion against God and his rule.[80] They sow doubt under the guise of a conversation, like the serpent in the garden asking Eve, "Did God actually say ... ?"[81] In recent years, we've seen this happen over and over again, and each time believers are left bewildered.

43

False Teaching, Itching Ears

In 2011, the Christian corner of the Internet cracked in two when a book by a well-known pastor suggested that the traditional understanding of God's eternal judgment is not only unhelpful but "devastating ... psychologically crushing ... terrifying and traumatizing and unbearable."[82] Perhaps, he argued, there isn't really eternal punishment for those who reject Christ; instead, maybe God continues to pursue them and their resistance eventually melts away in light of his tenacious love.[83] The firestorm surrounding this book drove it to the top of the sales charts and spawned probably hundreds of blog posts from across the spectrum of modern evangelicalism. Response books appeared seemingly within weeks.

There is no question some of the language in this debate got a little heated. What I found intriguing as the controversy unfolded, however, was the number of people—particularly those of a less conservative theological perspective—who were frustrated that this notion caused controversy at all. "Can we not restore unity?" they asked. "Does this really need to be such a big deal?"

In other words, "Why can't we live with our differences and all just get along?"

The argument centered on a truly significant issue, for if there is no eternal punishment, the entire gospel ultimately implodes. The problem isn't just a wrong understanding of the afterlife; it's a wrong understanding of God, attempting to prioritize his mercy over his justice. This argument represents a failure to understand God as he has revealed himself in the Scriptures; at worst,

it's outright rebellion against God's self-disclosure. It
was therefore right that many argued strenuously against
the book's position. Yet some remained committed to
a perceived ideal of unity as the greater good, and they
therefore would not or could not acknowledge the
dramatic shift that book made from orthodox teaching.

These are the doubters and deceived to whom we
must show mercy.

As tempting as it may be, we must not not overlook
the warnings from God's Word about false teachers
and ravenous wolves—they are there for our good and
growth in godliness, as painful as they are to read. These
truths should strike fear into our hearts. To say that some
among us—some who lead, teach, train, and write—are
not servants of Christ at all but actually (if often unwit-
tingly) servants of Satan seeking to destroy God's Church,
is deadly serious. But it's a charge to which all believers
must pay careful attention. God does not allow for a blasé
attitude toward false teaching or those who spread it.

So what should we do? These warnings do not
encourage modern day witch-hunts. Judgment belongs not
to us but to the Lord. It is Jesus's job "to execute judgment
on all and to convict all the ungodly of all their deeds of
ungodliness that they have committed in such an ungodly
way, and of all the harsh things that ungodly sinners have
spoken against him."[84] He will not allow his name to be
maligned nor his people be destroyed by damnable heresy.
We need not take his duties upon ourselves.

But we must be watchful. D. A. Carson offers good
counsel about how to do this:

If you find someone who has been a public teacher of Christianity for some time and who then gradually moves away from the centre of the faith, it sometimes takes a while to discern the nature of the drift.

When the first people to notice begin to wave a red flag, others say, "Oh, come on, you're being much too critical. After all, we trust this person; he's been such a huge help to us." It might take a very long time before many people clearly see how serious this drift is.

Such teachers, then, are traitors. They have turned their backs on what they once taught and defended, and so they have become treacherous.[85]

Our mission begins with discernment. We must know our Bibles well and hold fast to the truth we find there. We must search for and celebrate godly teachers. Pastors must shepherd and protect the flock. And the flock must work as well: "building yourselves up in your most holy faith and praying in the Holy Spirit, keep yourselves in the love of God, waiting for the mercy of our Lord Jesus Christ that leads to eternal life."[86]

A Framework for Contending

Clearly, a great many things are stacked against us if we desire to contend well and wisely. This is as it should be, for God wants us to cry out to him for assistance. As in all things, he is the one who ultimately gives the increase. Yet there are things we can and should do to prepare ourselves to be effective contenders.

If we will live up to our calling—if we will push through the complexity and messiness of contending in order to show mercy to those who doubt and are deceived, and if we will have the holy boldness to recognize and call out false teaching on essential issues when we see it—we must do two things:

1. We must take our faith as seriously as the New Testament authors do.
2. We must take false teaching as seriously as the New Testament authors do.

Jude calls this "keep[ing] yourselves in the love of God."[87] The apostle Paul calls it "keep[ing] a close watch on yourself and on the teaching."[88]

Everything you've read so far in this book was intended to lay the groundwork so that you can press forward in obeying these verses, armed with a clear understanding of their teaching and context. Now it's time to get a little more practical as we see how God equips us for the task in community.

Four
THE CLERGY

Called to Feed, Correct, and Protect

Growing up in a non-Christian family, I had all the usual ideas about church—the place is just stuffy, boring, and filled with hypocrites. But when Jesus saved me, he immediately brought me into community with other believers. As the church extended to my wife and me a great deal of love and patience, and as we began to re-learn life as followers of Christ, I quickly saw how wrong I had been. Church is amazing.

Of course, no local church is perfect—does anything go perfectly when you put a bunch of sinners in a room together? Nevertheless, local expressions of the Body of Christ are simply a gift from God. The local church is a principal means by which God sanctifies us, for in community we are formed more and more into the image of Christ.[89] It should be no surprise, then, that community is essential to contending.

In community, we honestly but safely work out some of the challenges to contending that we have seen so far in this book:

- Many professing Christians have trouble accepting that debate, disagreement, and even division in the face of false doctrine can ever be the better and wiser path, despite the fact that the New Testament affirms this in the clearest possible terms.
- Others maintain a tenuous grasp on the most primary matters of the Christian faith, effectively denying even the concept that doctrine can be false on the basis of Scripture.
- Meanwhile, all of us come at these issues with our individual predispositions, weaknesses, and blind spots.

In community, we address these challenges and take steps toward obeying Jude's command to contend for the faith. Jude tells us plainly that we must do it this way, working these things out among ourselves: "But you, beloved, building yourselves up in your most holy faith and praying in the Holy Spirit, keep yourselves in the love of God, waiting for the mercy of our Lord Jesus Christ that leads to eternal life."⁹⁰

The thrust of Jude's directive here is simple: *In order to contend faithfully, we must first live faithfully as Christians.* We "keep" ourselves in the love of God—we guard our hearts and minds from error—by being proactive about growing in our faith, and we do that in community. Without the pursuit of these goals through God's enabling grace, we will not grow in faithfulness. Without growth in faithfulness, we will not stand in the face of opposition. And if we cannot stand in the face of opposition, we will not be able to contend for the faith, either within our own hearts or outwardly for the sake of others. Indeed, instead of contending against heresy, we will be "tossed to and fro by the waves and carried about by every wind of doctrine."[91] Instead of showing mercy to those who doubt, we will crush our hearers under a weight of condemnation, using the Word of God as a sledgehammer rather than a scalpel.

All Christian are called to contend, in various ways and in the various roles to which God has called us. This requires us to take what is often the more difficult path, doing what doesn't come quite so naturally. When we contend—whether inwardly or outwardly—we act in faith and hope, trusting that as we obey God and cooperate with him, truth may prevail over error, obedience over disobedience, and godliness over sin. Contending takes the narrow way; it is not a path to travel alone. This, practically speaking, is why God gives us community. We gather in our local churches to praise the Lord Jesus corporately *and* to work out our faith practically, with "fear and trembling"[92] to the glory of God. He does not leave us to our own devices to figure out how to live faithfully. He gives us pastors and leaders to help guide us and fellow congregation members to walk alongside us on this journey of obedience to Christ and his Word. It's in this context that we contend for the faith—first (and continually) inwardly, and then (as necessary) outwardly.

To contend inwardly means preaching to ourselves and pursuing sanctification, but to contend outwardly means speaking the truth to others in love. This latter is one of the greatest acts of mercy we can perform—greater even than charity—for it holds out the hope of eternal blessing. To contend in this way is to humbly and confidently confront error and folly while calling the wayward to the truth of the gospel. It is to "have mercy on those who doubt; save others by snatching them out of the fire; to … show mercy with fear, hating even the garment stained by the flesh."[93] How can we ever hope to tackle such a huge task?

In this chapter and the next, we will focus on the ways God equips us for just this task in the local church. We begin by paying special attention to the role of pastors.

The Weight of Pastoral Ministry

The role of pastor within the local church is special and carries unique responsibility. The Bible is emphatic that pastoral ministry is a difficult calling—so much so that James writes, "Not many of you should become teachers, my brothers, for you know that we who teach will be judged with greater strictness."[94] At the same time, however, pastors are not a separate class of Christian. Indeed, as many have pointed out, the qualifications for elders[95] are what *all* believers should aspire to: each of us should strive to be above reproach in our conduct and reputation, self-controlled, respectable, hospitable, and humble, to name just a few. The Bible even draws a direct parallel between pastoring and the much more common role of fathering: The pastor "must manage his own household well, with all dignity keeping his children submissive, for if someone does not know how to manage his own household, how will he care for God's church?"[96]

Before becoming a father I didn't fully understand this parallel. A few years into parenthood, however, it began to click. As a father, my responsibility to my children is enormous, and I love them dearly. While I love to play with them, I don't serve my kids simply by being their jungle gym: I go to work to provide them with healthy food (even if they don't like it), I set appropriate boundaries and discipline them when they cross the line, and I do all I can to protect them from any kind of harm. I want to be a godly father who labors — who contends — for the sake of the bodies, minds, and souls of his children.

Do you see the spiritual parallels? These are the same three basic responsibilities, albeit in the spiritual sense, that a pastor is called to exercise toward his church members. As a good father serves his children, so a good pastor will serve and even contend for his church, and he will do that in three basic ways:

- Feeding
- Correcting
- Protecting

Good Pastors Feed God's People

The most important aspect of contending in pastoral ministry is a positive one — spiritually feeding God's people. Just as sheep need to be led to safe pasture where food and water can be found, we need to be continually led to the Word of God. The Reformers understood this well; in arranging their liturgy, they made the sermon the center-piece of the worship gathering. They knew there is nothing more important for us than to hear the Scriptures faithfully taught. This is the heritage of evangelical Protestants—it's at the heart of what it means to be "people of the Book."

Yet, despite its importance, faithful preaching has been on the decline in many places. Do you know of a church in which music or fellowship or drama or humor or video or clever stories have effectively replaced faithful preaching of the Bible as the very heart of the meeting? Every New Testament author would tell you this is a church in trouble. The Scriptures are emphatic on the centrality of the faithful proclamation of God's Word:

- Paul was eager to preach the gospel and his ambition was to make Christ's name known among those who had not heard.[97]
- Paul charges Timothy to "preach the word; be ready in season and out of season; reprove, rebuke, and exhort, with complete patience and teaching."[98]
- Jesus tells us that his purpose in coming was to preach: "I must preach the good news of the kingdom of God ... for I was sent for this purpose."[99]
- Jesus commanded the Apostles to preach the good news.[100]
- The Apostles were devoted "to prayer and to the ministry of the word."[101]

The command to feed God's people spiritually is most clearly spelled out in John 21:15–17, where we

see the risen Christ's restoration of Peter. Previously,
the proud apostle had put his foot in his mouth, boldly
proclaiming that he would never renounce Christ, even
at the cost of his own life. But when it actually came
time to be counted, Peter publicly denied his Lord, his
boldness melting away as he was questioned by various
onlookers.[102] A few days later, after Jesus returned from
the grave, he had business with Peter:

> When they had finished breakfast, Jesus said to Simon
> Peter, "Simon, son of John, do you love me more than
> these?" He said to him, "Yes, Lord; you know that I
> love you." He said to him, "Feed my lambs." He said
> to him a second time, "Simon, son of John, do you
> love me?" He said to him, "Yes, Lord; you know that
> I love you." He said to him, "Tend my sheep." He
> said to him the third time, "Simon, son of John, do
> you love me?" Peter was grieved because he said to
> him the third time, "Do you love me?" and he said to
> him, "Lord, you know everything; you know that I
> love you." Jesus said to him, "Feed my sheep."

In restoring Peter to service, Jesus asks him three
times, "Peter, do you love me? Do you love me more than
these other men? Do you love me?" Just as Peter denied
Jesus three times, so three times Jesus asks this question.
And each time Peter responds, "Lord, you know that I
love you." Now look at the response that this profes-
sion of love brings. Three times Jesus tells him, "Feed
my lambs.... Tend my sheep.... Feed my sheep." Jesus

is telling Peter that his responsibility as a leader in the Church—as an under-shepherd to the Good Shepherd—is to care for the needs of the people over whom Jesus has given him charge. As a pastor, this means he must direct them to the "green pastures" of the Word of God.

Consider the implications of this commission. If the pastor must "feed" us the Word, then he has a responsibility to preach the Scriptures clearly, not deliver a feel-good message that even a non-Christian could fully agree with. The pastor must devote himself to the consistent and clear proclamation of the message that Jesus himself characterized as a *sword*. Like the Apostles, he must be devoted to the ministry of the Word and committed to teaching sound doctrine to those under his care. And like a father who desires to help his children grow strong and healthy, he must ensure that we receive the "pure spiritual milk" of the Scriptures that allows them to "grow up into salvation."[103]

The Word of God is "able to make you wise for salvation through faith in Christ Jesus,"[104] and so it must be proclaimed. "All Scripture is breathed out by God and profitable for teaching, for reproof, for correction, and for training in righteousness,"[105] and so it must be taught. The living and active Word of God "[pierces] to the division of soul and of spirit, of joints and of marrow, and [discerns] the thoughts and intentions of the heart,"[106] and so it must be preached if we are to understand the desperate condition of our souls and the glorious promises of Christ. Proclaiming even the most difficult truths of Scripture to us as God's people ought not to be a mere duty for the pastor, but a positive delight.

Yet this kind of talk can strike a sour note in our day. In many places, a remarkably low view of preaching has taken hold. Especially in the self-centered culture of North America, many have replaced the full counsel of God with little more than morality tales and exhortations to "feed yourself." While it's true that every believer ought to be proactive in growing in godliness, tasting for ourselves that the Lord is good,[107] pastoral exhortations to feed ourselves don't actually encourage us in this, and may do little more than feed our self-reliance. I can't prove this, but my sense is that the preachers who regularly urge their flocks to feed themselves are typically not doing a very good job of feeding from the pulpit in the first place.

Someone who specializes in giving nice talks or delivering cute messages is not functioning as a gospel herald and under-shepherd of Christ. The apostle Paul serves as our example of a faithful pastor when we read his final words to the Ephesian elders:

> You yourselves know how I lived among you the whole time from the first day that I set foot in Asia, serving the Lord with all humility and with tears and with trials that happened to me through the plots of the Jews; how I did not shrink from declaring to you anything that was profitable, and teaching you in public and from house to house, testifying both to Jews and to Greeks of repentance toward God and of faith in our Lord Jesus Christ. And now, behold, I am going to Jerusalem, constrained by the Spirit, not knowing what will happen to me there, except that the Holy Spirit

testifies to me in every city that imprisonment and afflictions await me. But I do not account my life of any value nor as precious to myself, if only I may finish my course and the ministry that I received from the Lord Jesus, to testify to the gospel of the grace of God. And now, behold, I know that none of you among whom I have gone about proclaiming the kingdom will see my face again. Therefore I testify to you this day that I am innocent of the blood of all, for I did not shrink from declaring to you the whole counsel of God.[108]

Paul did not "shrink from declaring … anything that was profitable." He said rightfully that he was "innocent of the blood of all," and the reason was that he "did not shrink from declaring … the whole counsel of God." He had fulfilled his duty to them: he had proclaimed the gospel in its fullness, and his hands were clean. This calling and mandate stands even today for everyone who calls himself pastor, preacher, or teacher in the church. The responsibility is too great and the cost too high to do any less than preach the full counsel of God.

We who are God's people need to be led to "green pastures." We need to be shown that the depths of the Word of God are limitless. That's what good preaching does—and that's what Christ's sheep need if we will grow and mature in holiness so that we can contend for the faith. As R. C. Sproul puts it so well:

When the sheep of Christ are fed, nurtured, and filled with the strength of Christ and of His word, they become a mighty army turned loose on the world. Babies have almost no influence in a culture. Before they can turn the world upside down, they have to grow up, they have to become mature, and that happens as they are fed the Word of God. Nothing less will do.[109]

Good Pastors Correct God's People

Along with feeding God's people, the pastor must also correct us when we stray into error. Again, this is where the exhortation to preach the whole counsel of God is so critical. Remember that Paul writes that "all Scripture is ... profitable for teaching, for reproof, for correction, and for training in righteousness." The package of "reproof plus correction" is critical to our understanding of how the pastor contends for God's people. To offer reproof means to confront error, declaring in no uncertain terms that some particular idea, attitude, or action is wrong. But reproof is insufficient in itself. Reproof identifies the problem but doesn't clarify the solution. The "Don't do that" must be followed by, "Instead, do this, and here's why."

Indeed, when Paul addressed the Corinthians in the face of their rampant failures to practice self-control, he didn't stop at "Quit it!" or even merely "Now try this" and so promote mere morality. He *began* with reproof but then moved on to Christ-centered correction, calling them back to a holy and self-controlled life and pleading with them to recall the grace of Christ. Paul emphatically reminded the Corinthians that they were a people purchased by Christ, that God was at work among them, and that they were to live in light of that truth. He reproved them for their error, but then he also corrected it for the sake of Christ. Faithful pastoring and preaching must do likewise.

Error will certainly try to seep into every congregation, for the world and the flesh and the devil are permanently opposed to the progress of the gospel. The pastor who cannot discern actual error, or who is unwilling both to reprove and correct it when necessary, badly misses the mark. As Paul warned both the Corinthians and the Galatians, "A little leaven leavens the whole lump."[110] Uncorrected error only leads to greater error among the flock.

Good Pastors Protect God's People

We have seen that pastors must *feed* God's people with the Word, encouraging us to grow spiritually. When we go astray pastors must *reprove* our wayward behavior and attitudes, and then bring *correction* by proclaiming to us the grace that Christ offers for the restoration and renewal of character and heart. But alongside these responsibilities is the pastor's call to *protect* us from error and those who promote it. A pastor protects his flock by seeking to prevent the introduction or spread of false teaching in the church.[111]

Recall that although Jude was eager to write about "our common salvation," he was unable to act on this preference because of the looming threat of false teaching. Instead, he "found it *necessary* to write appealing to you to contend for the faith." Pastors are called to wisely and prayerfully discern truth from error in order to protect their congregations from the infection of false teaching, but because there is always an abundance of error seeking to infiltrate the church, pastors must also discern when a particular false teaching is a threat to his specific congregation. C. J. Mahaney offered three questions to help pastors make this determination.

- Does this teaching threaten the gospel?
- What is the condition of your flock?
- Does this teaching threaten the gospel in the church where I serve?[112]

Does This Teaching Threaten the Gospel?

It cannot be said too often: if a particular teaching contradicts the gospel, it must not be allowed to take hold in a local church. Sometimes the contradictions are obvious, but other teachings are more subtle—they may have "crept in unnoticed." Some of the errors that can creep in gradually include

- Teaching that suggests evangelism isn't important because God is sovereign (a manifestation of what is often called hyper-Calvinism).
- Teaching that questions the severity of sin and man's need for justification by faith in Christ alone (Pelagianism or semi-pelagianism).[113]

- Teaching that questions the extent of God's knowledge of and sovereignty over all things (open theism).
- Teaching that obscures Christ's work of freeing his people from bondage to sin by portraying it instead as a call to free the oppressed of this world from temporal concerns (liberation theology).[114]
- Teaching that confuses the distinction between God and his creation (Christian mysticism).

If a particular teaching does *not* threaten the gospel, the pastor may *prefer* to address it or *choose* to address it, but if it *does* threaten the gospel, and it passes the test of the next two questions, a pastor is obligated before God to refute this error in order to protect his flock.

What is the Condition of Your Flock?

This question speaks to the spiritual condition and pre-paredness of a given church body.[115] The pastor needs to ask first whether his church is theologically equipped to contend for the faith in a particular area, and second, if the church is not so equipped, whether it needs to be?

At the congregational level, some churches are simply more prone or less prone to a particular false teaching. A church with a long and faithful history of solid biblical teaching is not likely to be threatened, for example, by prosperity theology or word-of-faith teaching, even if the high-profile church up the street teaches one of these errors.

Within a particular church, however, a finer level of analysis may be in order. Those individuals who are spiritually anemic and not well-grounded in the Scriptures are far less likely to see the need for thoughtful contending, even as they are more prone to buying into teaching that threatens the gospel. But those individuals who understand the truth and beauty of the gospel and who are growing in their knowledge of and affection for God's Word are well equipped to recognize false teaching and reject it out of hand. They are also readily able to understand why a pastor would address such an error if it does begin to creep into a congregation, and they will probably wholeheartedly support any such effort.

This question, therefore, is all about whether a particular church, or a group of people within that church, are likely to fall prey to a given false teaching should it begin to creep in.

Does This Teaching Threaten the Gospel in the Church Where I Serve?

This is the bottom line. After the two questions above have been answered, a pastor can weigh whether he ought to publicly address a particular false teaching within a particular church at a particular time. If a real threat appears to exist, it must be addressed.

Paul took context into consideration when he contended. He warned Timothy of Hymenaeus, Alexander, and Philetus, calling them men who had made a wreck of their faith by departing from the truth. Paul did this because the teaching and example of these men could have damaged Timothy's ministry in Ephesus.[116] But Paul did not warn Titus of these three. Similarly, when

Jesus warned of the Nicolaitans, whose works he hated and against whom he promised to make war if they did not repent,[117] he did so only to the Ephesians (applauding their positive rejection) and Pergamum (condemning their foolish acceptance). He said nothing of the Nicolaitans to the other five churches he addressed.

These biblical examples legitimize a common-sense observation: Not every threat to the gospel is necessarily a threat to a particular church at a particular time. "Not all national and international conversations are immediately applicable to my church," explains Mahaney. "One must do this wisely and strategically, not giving undo attention to something outside the context of your local church."

<u>What about naming names?</u> Is it ever right and biblical for a pastor to warn against a specific teacher? The short answer is yes. We just saw how Paul and the Lord Jesus singled out particular individuals or movements. They certainly named names. At the same time, this is obviously an area where discernment is required.

It is no small thing to declare someone a false teacher, and this should never be done without substantial evidence. A single out-of-context quotation, for example, does not prove someone is a heretic. At the same time, some teachings threaten the gospel, but their leading spokesmen have no influence within a given church. Here, naming names would be more like gossip than contending for the faith. But if a consistent body of teaching presented over time strongly points in a particular problematic direction, and if a particular proponent of the false doctrine has a hearing in the church, that is another matter.

In sum, if a pastor feels confident that a particular teaching

- genuinely threatens the gospel
- and his church is vulnerable to this teaching
- and his church is being exposed to this teaching

then he is required before God to protect his people through feeding and/or correcting.

- He may need to feed his people, teaching them what they need to know so that they will see this false doctrine for what it is and resist it.
- He may need to reprove and correct anyone within his church who has begun to embrace the false doctrine.
- He may need to publicly identify any leading representatives of the false teaching who may be gaining influence within the church, whether through books, podcasts, online sermons, radio broadcasts, local meetings, or some other way.

Whether overtly false or subtly deceptive, teachings that threaten the gospel in our local churches must be addressed for the spiritual health and vitality of the congregation. Teaching contrary to sound doctrine cannot be tolerated but must be rebuked and expunged. This is much of what it means for a pastor to contend for the flock.

A Plea for Prayer, Love, and Patience

Few of us are in positions of official church leadership. But we are all members of the Body. That's why we must have a basic understanding of what it means for pastors to contend for the flock.

Perhaps you feel that your pastors are doing an outstanding job of this. That's wonderful, and you would do well to pause right now and thank God for the gift they are to your congregation. But maybe you have a different opinion of your leaders. Again, nothing could be more appropriate than for you to pray for any leaders who you feel are especially in need of God's guidance. But whatever your situation—if your pastor is one who faithfully feeds, corrects, and protects the congregation, or one who struggles to do so—here are a few ways you can apply what you've read.

Support Your Pastor Wherever Possible and in Every Way Possible

Your pastor needs your prayers and encouragement more than you realize (and probably more than he lets on).[118] If you're concerned about your pastor's performance in this area, the best thing you can do is pray that God would bring conviction and a desire to change where needed.

Be Respectful in All You Do

Christian, you are called not only to "obey your leaders and submit to them, for they are keeping watch over your souls," but do so in a way that would make their oversight joyful.[119] At the same time, be willing to approach your pastors as you would anyone else who you think needs biblical encouragement and possibly correction.

Pastors really are just people. Your pastor is a sinner subject to the same frailties and potential for blindness as anyone else. Therefore, while you must respect his calling, his office, his maturity, and his experience, do not be afraid to ask pointed, respectful questions or make helpful observations grounded in Scripture.

If you are the least bit uncertain that any concerns you may have about a particular church leader are valid, then before you speak to that leader, discreetly ask a small number of trusted friends to test your discernment. Limit these counselors to people you are confident you can trust to keep your questions to themselves. It is essential that you do nothing that would tend to create factions or divisions within the church. If you then remain concerned that your pastor or pastors are genuinely missing the mark with respect to some central component of their ministry, go directly to them and humbly explain your concerns.

Know When to Stay and When to Go

What if your concerns are valid but your pastor will not hear them? What do you do if you try your best to support your pastor but in the end find that you cannot? Entire books have been written on this subject[120] and for good reason—it's tricky. When you legitimately can no longer support your current pastor, especially when the issue is something significant, you need to leave. But do not just leave—leave well.

Search for a local church that is pastored more closely to a biblical model. If you plan to leave a church, begin looking for another church shepherded by a qualified man who clearly loves God's people and God's Word. Search the Scriptures and read good books to find the marks of a healthy church.[121] Talk to members of a congregation you think you might want to join to learn what they appreciate about the church and how God is using it. If at all possible, avoid a scenario where you leave without a place to land.

Respectfully withdraw from your current congregation. Finish your ministry commitments as best as you are able. Request an exit meeting with your pastor so you can explain your reasons for leaving. If at all possible, avoid just disappearing from the congregation.

Strive to speak well of your previous church when moving on to the next. It can be tempting to tear down a church or pastor, especially if your exit hasn't been as clean as you would prefer or if you have sustained serious spiritual injuries in the process. Regardless of your experiences, take these words from the apostle Paul seriously: "Let all bitterness and wrath and anger and clamor and slander be put away from you, along with all malice."[122] Gossip, slander, and any other behaviors that create division are forbidden for the Christian. If we let our pain or frustration turn into bitterness, we'll be more inclined to use divisive and destructive language. Therefore prayerfully strive to be gracious in how you speak of your previous church and avoid unnecessarily negative comparisons.

If you want to contend, you need community, and pastors play a critical role in helping believers do that well. "Keep a close watch on yourself and on the teaching…. for by so doing you will save both yourself and your hearers," Paul commanded Timothy, and so commands leaders today as well.[123] Where pastors fail to faithfully teach and equip their congregations, God's people will be left unprepared to contend. But those who faithfully feed, correct, and protect God's people, submitting themselves and their congregations to God's Word, will not see their efforts put to shame as believers join in the task of keeping themselves "in the love of God."

Five
THE
CONGREGATION

Called to Build Up, Persevere, and Wait

One of the many reasons my wife and I love our local church is that the leaders understand what's necessary to make disciples. They realize, for example, that there's a limit to how much practical discipleship can take place during the Sunday worship gathering or the occasional class, as important as these things are. Even the most exemplary preaching and teaching isn't enough to keep someone truly growing.

Remember Jude's call: "keep *yourselves* in the love of God."[124] Jude tells us we must be *active participants in growing in our faith*. If we are to mature as disciples, fully equipped to contend, individual effort is required. We need to own our faith, to "work out [our] own salvation"[125] as we take responsibility for our growth in knowing and trusting the Lord.

Jude is telling us that if we are to contend faithfully, we must live faithfully. He isolates three things that will achieve that end: "But you, beloved, building yourselves up in your

most holy faith and praying in the Holy Spirit, keep yourselves in the love of God, waiting for the mercy of our Lord
Jesus Christ that leads to eternal life."[126] That is, to "keep"
ourselves in the love of God we should guard our hearts
and minds from error by pursuing three critical goals:

1. Being built up in faith
2. Persevering in prayer
3. Waiting for the Lord's future mercy[127]

These are the nitty-gritty elements of growing in our
faith. All three are vital.

Build Up Your Faith with the Bible

"The Bible can be so boring." "The Bible can be so hard to
understand."

Probably every Christian has felt this way at one
time or another. But such wicked ideas only eat away at
our faith. Would God reveal his will to his people in a
way that's impenetrable to the average person? Would he
present eternal truth in a way that doesn't captivate the
heart and mind?

If we come to Scripture in faith, seeing every word as
inspired, as living and powerful and active ... if we come
to the Bible prayerfully asking for illumination ... if we
come to the Bible in the way God encourages us to and
expects us to, we will not find his book boring or nearly so
difficult to understand. Instead, we will find it life-giving.

I'm not saying this is always easy. Certainly some passages of Scripture are less appealing or harder to understand, or they don't go down quite as readily as others. The challenge, then, is to take these sections as seriously as the passages we love the most. Rather than pretend the difficult passages aren't there or don't matter as much, we should engage with them, wrestling with the truth they present and searching other passages of Scripture for additional illumination.

Let's face it. In the Internet age we are frequently tempted to believe that we don't really need to think very deeply about anything. Shouldn't the fix be just a few clicks or taps away? Hasn't somebody figured this out so a quick, simple answer can be handed to us on a silver platter? *Whatever it is, give it to me efficiently, please, and preferably with a great user interface; I have things to do. Come on, this the 21st century!*

But the hard truth is that if we fail to take time to think deeply about the unsearchable, wonderful, endless depths of the Word of God—even the difficult passages—it's like turning off a tap or closing a door. We cut ourselves off from unique opportunities, robbing ourselves of rich possibilities including a deeper love for God, a more profound transformation of our hearts and minds, a more thorough shaping of our character, and a richer filling of our spirits. When Jude commands us to "build yourselves up in your most holy faith," he's talking about growing strong in our understanding—and this is impossible without faithful, consistent time in the Bible.[128]

As D. A. Carson writes:

In a world where there are many false ideas—many deceptive, selfish, and anti-God ideas—what must we do to get orientated toward God himself? We go to God's Word – we hold on to the Bible. We desperately need to think God's thoughts after him.... [Paul] writes to the church in Rome and tells them not to be conformed to the world, but to be transformed by the renewing of their minds (see Romans 12:1–2). And that means we must hold on to the Bible, not as a magic book, but one that teaches us how to think and what to think.... [If] we understand what this gospel is, and look at all of the world around us out of the framework of this gospel and this book, then we are able to withstand the subtle allure of passing fancies that drive us away from the God who is our Maker, Redeemer and Judge. Hold on to the Bible.[129]

Building ourselves up in the faith, which means (at least in part) growing strong doctrinally, requires us to hold on to the Bible. The absence of a consistent devotional life is not necessarily a mark of a reprobate, but if you're not engaging the Scriptures on a fairly consistent basis, you should take seriously the possibility that there is something fundamentally wrong with your walk. Every word of Scripture is "profitable for teaching, for reproof, for correction, and for training in righteousness," so as we hold onto God's Word, we will be "equipped for every good work."[130] The intake of Scripture—through reading, study, and/or meditation—is simply necessary if we are to continue being built up in our most holy faith. The alternative is not stability or stasis but actual decline, as our faith is gradually and inevitably broken down by the endless drumbeat of the world, the flesh, and the devil. There is no standing still in the Christian life.

Regular personal interaction with the Scriptures must be a priority for the Christian. Nothing else can "make you wise for salvation."[131]

Build Up Your Faith with Good Books

Without taking anything away from the primacy of Scripture, we would be foolish to ignore good books written by faithful believers.[132] In these books we see how other saints have wrestled with the deep things of God. We see their struggles and their joys as they engage the truths of Scripture, and we thus gain a larger vision of the Christian faith than our personal experience could provide on its own.

Many excellent books from Christians of past generations have withstood the test of time and are available today in various formats. This is in addition to solid contemporary authors whose language and writing style may be more accessible. Modern authors can also help us better understand the unique aspects of present-day challenges to the Christian life. Having a group of theologically solid "literary mentors," whether contemporary or already with the Lord, can be a chief means by which God shapes you into a disciple of Christ.

Again, books and commentaries should never replace

the Word of God as your primary focus. Moreover, it is neither wise nor helpful to your soul to get in the habit of running to someone else's understanding of Scripture until you have first grappled on your own with a particular topic or section of the Bible. Through Christian books, however, believers can genuinely help "build up one another in the faith," whether across the miles or across the centuries.

Build Up Your Faith by Persevering in Prayer

Prayer also plays a critical role in guarding our hearts and minds. "Beloved ... praying in the Holy Spirit, keep yourselves in the love of God," Jude writes. What does Jude mean by "praying in the Holy Spirit"? Tom Schreiner suggests he is likely speaking of "the ordinary prayer that should be part of the warp and the woof of the Christian life."[133]

Such ordinary prayer is an extraordinary thing. In prayer we set aside our own agendas and pray according to the leading of the Holy Spirit. Because the Spirit is one with the Father and the Son, he will always lead us toward prayers that are for our good, that glorify God, and that further the gospel. What better way to guard our hearts and minds against error than to continually align them with God's work in the earth as the Spirit leads us in prayer?

Given the weight that Jude puts on prayer in this verse, we would be wise to take a moment to evaluate our personal practice of prayer—not just the frequency, but the content and method. There are many helpful books, approaches, teachings, and techniques pertaining to prayer, but the best counsel I've seen (which also happens to be simple and straightforward) comes from Martin Luther.

Luther spent years developing his prayer life, seeing prayer as the "daily business of a Christian." In his little book *The Way to Pray*, he offered two critical secrets to a healthy prayer life. First, when your prayer life is feeling cold and joyless, turn to the Lord's Prayer, the Ten Commandments, and the Apostles' Creed. Pray through them, personally applying each line and focusing on instruction, thanksgiving, confession, and petition. Second, set and maintain specific times of prayer:

> It is a good thing to let prayer be the first business in the morning and the last at night. Guard yourself carefully against those false, deluding ideas that tell you, *Wait a little while. I will pray in an hour; first I must attend to this or that.* Such thoughts get you away from prayer into other affairs, which so hold your attention and involve you that nothing comes out of prayer for that day.[134]

We pray more effectively by determining the time and place in which to pray and sticking to it. Don't build prayer into your life but build your life around prayer. After all, "Believers cannot keep themselves in God's love without depending on him by petitioning him in prayer. Love for God cannot be sustained without a relationship with him, and such a relationship is nurtured by prayer."[135]

In addition to personal prayer, the Scriptures frequently depict prayer as a communal activity:

- On the night of his arrest, Jesus told Peter, James, and John, "Pray that you may not enter into temptation."[136]
- The early church, before the coming of the Holy Spirit, prayed together.[137]
- Peter and John went to pray at the Temple together.[138]
- The apostles devoted themselves to prayer (together and individually).[139]
- When Peter was arrested, the church prayed earnestly to God on his behalf.[140]
- James tells us to pray for one another.[141]

Prayer, whether personal or communal, guards our hearts and minds and commits our efforts to the Lord. And, perhaps most pertinent to our focus on contending for the faith outwardly, prayer helps guard our tongues.

As we saw in chapter three, too many words eventually spread evil. Error has a way of confronting us unexpectedly, for sin and our Enemy know the power of the surprise attack. In these moments, being too hasty with unwise or emotional words can actually be the worst kind of response: "There is one whose rash words are like sword thrusts, but the tongue of the wise brings healing."[142]

So we must remember, "Death and life are in the power of the tongue, and those who love it will eat its fruits."[143] When we are tempted to address error simply by reacting, let us instead pray for wisdom and understanding, that any words the Spirit might lead us to speak would be words of life, not death. If we are to contend well, we ought to pray in the Spirit that he would direct our words and use them for God's glory.

The Essential Role of the Church Community

With a couple of exceptions, so far in this chapter we have addressed our personal relationship with the Lord, something that by definition happens mostly in private. But this chapter title assumes that the congregation as a collective body is essential to the work of contending, and that's because the overall tenor of Jude's letter focuses on community. He does not write as if we are *isolated* individuals. When he says "keep *yourselves* in the love of God" there is *a people* in view, believers who stand before the Lord as individuals, yet who equally stand *with* one another as children of the Father, members of the flock, and fellow sojourners. Both perspectives are vital to walking out our faith biblically.

The New Testament makes it abundantly clear that while the personal component of our faith is primary, we do this Christian life *together*. We are individuals before God, yet collectively we form his church, his bride. The duality here is deeply profound, even echoing the fact that we serve a God who is himself one in three. But that is a discussion well beyond the scope of this book. For now, let's just say that we work out our own salvation at the individual level and the collective level in our local church *as part of a single process.*

Knowing the Bible, reading good books, praying, and (the subject of the next section) even exercising faith in God's future mercy—just like most other aspects of the Christian life, these find essential expression as solo activities, yet they are never intended to be *exclusively* solo activities. Bring any one of them into a live community context and they take on a different character, one that is complementary and additive and helpful and absolutely necessary to the kind of Christian life Jude is exhorting us to pursue.

Furthermore, Christian community also includes some things that cannot be done alone. These are primarily the ways we love and serve one another, echoing the fact that Christ loved and served us. These are the "one anothers" of the Christian life, practically manifested in things like spiritual conversation, sharing your struggles, encouraging and praying for one another, giving people rides, serving on ministry teams, helping with service projects, offering hospitality, preparing meals for one another—all the things that contribute to an actual shared life. These can create a richness of community that is uniquely Christian, testifying to the world and to one another of the love of Jesus.[144]

Of course, we live in a day when virtual communities, mediated by technology, are sometimes portrayed as equal or even preferable to actual, local communities, which for Christians means the local church. The only sober, biblical view is to see that while virtual communities can at times be beneficial, we should never see them as coming anywhere near replacing or superseding the local church.

In sum, taking *personal* ownership of our faith must include an active role in *community*. Growing in godliness is never exclusively a solitary activity. We need community if we really are to live out our faith. We need other believers alongside us to encourage, challenge, and sometimes correct us. Our participation in the local church is itself an act of contending for the faith as we grow together in the grace and knowledge of God.

Build Up Your Faith with the Promise of Future Mercy

We end this chapter by considering Jude's final means of "building up" in which he calls us to "[wait] for the mercy of our Lord Jesus Christ that leads to eternal life." Here, he speaks not of a present reality but of an expectation, a promise that is yet to be fulfilled but still certain. We wait for the final mercy we will receive at the coming of the Lord—the fulfillment of the promise of eternal life. This is the same hope we see throughout the New Testament:

- We "[wait] for our blessed hope, the appearing of the glory of our great God and Savior Jesus Christ."[145]
- From heaven, "we await a Savior, the Lord Jesus Christ, who will transform our lowly body to be like his glorious body, by the power that enables him even to subject all things to himself."[146]
- We "who have the firstfruits of the Spirit ... wait eagerly for adoption as sons, the redemption of our bodies."[147]
- "Through the Spirit, by faith, we ourselves eagerly wait for the hope of righteousness."[148]

The hope that guards us is that of Christ's return, when he will usher in the new creation, glorify our bodies, fully cleanse and purify our hearts, and put a final end to sin and death. This blessed hope both sustains us and equips us to contend to the glory of God, that we might be faithful witnesses of Christ before a watching world.

What do we do, then, as we wait for the full appearance of God's mercy? How do we do that waiting? Those who wait for mercy show mercy, as Jude tells us in the next verses: "Have mercy on those who doubt; save others by snatching them out of the fire; to others show mercy with fear, hating even the garment stained by the flesh." What do we see here?

- For people, we should have nothing but mercy. Because of God's promise to us in Jesus Christ, there is hope for any living soul.
- For the outworkings of sin, we should have nothing but hatred (as well as a sober, holy fear of sin's power to tempt and deceive us). This is also a form of mercy, for we know by God's same promise in Jesus that one day all traces of sin and its corruption will be banished forever.

In contending, we stand firm *on* sound doctrine and we stand *against* false doctrine. But contending is about more than right knowledge. Equally important is *how* we contend: the purest mercy toward those who doubt and are being led astray, and the purest hatred toward sin.

That is why Jude reminds us to wait upon the coming

of Christ. Because we are living in anticipation of the mercy we will receive at the return of Christ in glory, we are able to extend that same mercy to those who grow weak in faith. "Mercifully pull them back," Gundry writes. "Don't push them over [into apostasy] out of dismay over their attraction to the heretics."[149]

This is what contending should look within a church family. We correct and admonish one another so that those who are being led astray may be reclaimed and restored. We enter the fray with care and caution, praying for wisdom and self-control, desiring to speak the truth in love, showing mercy to those who doubt.

Six
THE CONCLUSION

What Contending Really Means

I had been home from work just a few minutes one evening when Emily said, "So, Abigail tells me they were doing yoga in gym class today." For us, this simple sentence was pregnant with implications.

Yoga is a hot-button issue for many Christians in the West. Opinions are all over the place. In fact, Emily and I had spent two years doing research and studying the Scriptures before coming to a shared conviction that yoga is incompatible with consistent Christian practice. So when we learned that our daughter was expected to do yoga in school, it raised a real issue for us. Because Abigail is in public school, we fully expected that at some point we would have to talk with her teachers about one thing or another—we just didn't expect it to happen a few weeks into kindergarten.

As we looked at this situation, we saw we had two options:

1. **Ignore it.** Set aside our convictions, allowing us to avoid a conversation that would probably be awkward and might well get us and our daughter labeled as weirdos.

2. **Address it.** Be open with the school about our discomfort and concerns, and ask that Abigail be excused from doing yoga.

We knew we had to choose option two; in our view, our convictions about yoga and our parental responsibilities toward our daughter qualified this as an issue about God and his nature, a primary issue that could not be ignored. So I sat down with Abigail's teacher and tried to be gracious and clear. The conversation was definitely awkward, and I'm not quite sure how we are now perceived, but her teacher was gracious in return and Abigail is no longer doing yoga.

The point of this story, of course, is not yoga. It's that there are uncomfortable things we must all be prepared to do — and do in a very Christian way — if we are really going to take our faith seriously. And that, at its most basic level, is what it means to contend. Recall our working definition:

> *Contending must be understood and exercised*
> *as an act of mercy toward those who doubt*
> *and those who have been deceived,*
> *regardless of whether they claim faith in Christ.*

In speaking to Abigail's teacher I was contending for the faith on at least four fronts:

1. Digging up seeds of doubt and deception about the nature of God that Abigail's participation in yoga may have planted in her heart, and/or reducing the likelihood that such seeds would be planted in the future.

2. Demonstrating the seriousness of the gospel along with some of its content to Abigail's teacher and, by extension, to the school administration.
3. Serving my wife by leading and protecting our family.
4. Challenging and encouraging myself in the faith by stepping out into an area of discomfort for the sake of the gospel.

Jude uses this powerful, almost aggressive word *contend* to remind us that the Christian life isn't a passive one. We don't just "go with the flow" and hope that we and those whom we are called to love and serve wind up godlier than we began. After all, the Christian life is a *war*, one not fought "against flesh and blood, but ... against the spiritual forces of evil in the heavenly places."[150]

Jude wants us to be serious about our faith, so he directs us toward a costly spiritual aggressiveness that is nevertheless grounded in mercy, and he gives us some vital ways in which this applies to church life because of the insidious nature of "hidden reefs." Jude wants to bring the essential truths of the faith to bear in all areas. He wants us to submit every thought to the authority of Scripture, speak every word in light of the grace given to us in the gospel, and focus every action to the glory of our Triune God.

Consider these examples.

• When a single person makes a decision to say no to a particular TV program or video game because it will rob him of joy in the nature and character of God, this is contending for the faith *inwardly*.

- When in mercy this person encourages a Christian friend to think along similar lines, he is contending for the faith *outwardly*. Both actions help strengthen the body of Christ.
- When in love and mercy a wife confronts her husband about his struggles with anger, challenging him to grow in his character, she is contending for the faith.
- When a husband offers gracious encouragement to his wife in order to build her up in her work, he is contending for the faith.
- When a family chooses to sacrifice home ownership and income in order to have one parent at home, they are contending for the faith.
- When parents teach and discipline their children in light of the gospel, they are contending for the faith.
- When a pastor believes the full counsel of God is so necessary that he refuses to gloss over a hard passage, he is contending for the faith.
- When a worship leader chooses music that displays God's transcendent nature, he is contending for the faith.
- When a student lovingly confronts a friend from youth group whose lifestyle is increasingly worldly, she is contending for the faith.
- When an employee encourages his openly Christian-but-disconnected-from-community employer to join a local church, he is contending for the faith.
- When an actor refuses a career-making role because it requires her to compromise on her values, she is contending for the faith.

You get the picture. All these are examples of what it looks like to contend for the faith. None of them represent the path of least resistance. None of them are easy. But if we are going to defend the centrality of Scripture, the nature and character of God, and the truth of the gospel, actions like these are necessary.

The Challenge of Contending

How can we best do this? Here are two things to remember.

<u>Demonstrate humility: Christians can and must contend without being contentious.</u> Just like Jude's audience, we have been called by, purchased by, and kept for Jesus Christ. Whatever insights we may have into Scripture are not due to our superior intellectual or moral attainments — they are gifts from God meant to bring him glory and honor.[151] This is why, in all our contending, we must reject "an unhealthy craving for controversy,"[152] and instead "be ready for every good work, to speak evil of no one, to avoid quarreling, to be gentle, and to show perfect courtesy toward all people."[153]

The contentious person is simply looking for a fight. He " stirs up division ... is warped and sinful; he is self-condemned."[154] When Paul says in those same verses that we should have nothing to do with such a person, it follows that we must not be like him. Instead, we must count others as better and more important than ourselves.[155] While this is clearly a struggle for many Christians, to contend biblically is nevertheless to illu-minate where unbiblical perspectives fall short without condemning, demonizing, or pretending to be superior to those who hold such views.

Love others: Contending is not about making doctrine more important than people. Jesus' message to the church at Ephesus is instructive for us on this point. In Revelation 2, we read:

> I know your works, your toil and your patient endurance, and how you cannot bear with those who are evil, but have tested those who call themselves apostles and are not, and found them to be false. I know you are enduring patiently and bearing up for my name's sake, and you have not grown weary.[156]

Let's trace the history here. The Ephesians had been warned by Paul in Acts 20:29 that fierce wolves would arise from among their own number. This is exactly what Jude warned against: anti-Christian influences infiltrating the church membership. Thus forewarned, the Ephesians had tested their teachers and, by contending for the faith, had succeeded in resisting the lure of false teaching, keeping their doctrine pure. Praise God for this! Oh, that we would have more numbered among us who show that kind of care toward the teaching we allow into our midst.

But Jesus' message to the Ephesians doesn't stop with that encouragement. He follows it with a rebuke:

> But I have this against you, that you have abandoned the love you had at first. Remember therefore from where you have fallen; repent, and do the works you

did at first. If not, I will come to you and remove your lampstand from its place, unless you repent.[157]

The Ephesians deeply loved the truth of the gospel, and that love overflowed toward "all the saints," giving the apostle Paul cause to rejoice.[158] Yet, it seems that despite their rock-solid doctrine and their wealth of love for one another, their hearts had become cold to the truths that had once burned so warm within them. Sam Storms writes:

> What we see in the church at Ephesus, therefore, was how their desire for orthodoxy and the exclusion of error had created a climate of suspicion and mistrust in which brotherly love could no longer flourish. Their eager pursuit of truth had to some degree soured their affections one for another. It's one thing not to "bear with those who are evil" (Revelation 2:2), but it's another thing altogether when that intolerance carries over to your relationship with other Christ-loving Christians![159]

The Ephesians were contending, yes, but without grace and love—and to Christ, that very imbalance represented a serious violation of what it means to be his followers. This should serve as a strong warning for us as we consider how we approach contending for the faith. We must not forget that there are *people* involved in every debate, both "those who are evil" and those who are, as Storms puts it, "Christ-loving Christians."

We often see those with whom we disagree as something close to demons, when it's much more likely that they have been duped. To miss this is to cause two great harms:

1. We disserve those who need a Savior.
2. We dishonor and misrepresent the Savior who has positioned and prepared us to serve.

There is a tension in contending that requires us to uphold both people *and* doctrine. We cannot contend without love for people any more than we can contend without a love for truth. Consider Sam Storms again: "Doctrinal precision is absolutely necessary. But it isn't enough. May God grant us grace to love others with no less fervor than we love the truth."[160]

The Delight of Contending

So we see that in the end, contending is a powerful and accurate metaphor for living the Christian life—a way of envisioning what it means to *be* intentionally Christian. Jude uses this aggressive, physical term to underscore that the Christian life is active, not passive. We must pay attention to what's going on around us and live in a doctrinally aware manner. We must lean into what faith is all about and bring those truths to bear in all areas of life because we really are in a war.

Contending is therefore not an add-on to living the

Christian life. It is not some distinct function or special mode. It's just being serious about our faith.

No area of life is left untouched by the call to contend. Nothing can be compartmentalized or hidden in a corner. Contending takes place in our hearts, in our marriages, in our vocations, in our hobbies, in the culture, in the church. We should be so sold-out, so uncompromising about the essentials of the faith that we'll put aside whatever gets in the way.

Each of us, at various stages of life, will be called to say "no" to certain things for the sake of Christ and the good of others, even when it seems much simpler and more satisfying in the short term to say "yes." But to walk closely with Jesus is worth far more than any worldly comfort. Unbelieving family members won't understand your decisions. Even some believing friends may struggle at times. But contending is the cost of discipleship.

If we love anything—our comfort, our reputations, even our families—more than we love Christ, we will fail to contend for the faith.[161] We will fail to truly live the Christian life as Jude calls us to. We must understand that contending is divisive because Jesus is divisive, and that adds friction to a life that we desperately want to be smooth and easy. The world wants us to be quiet and play nice. Enemies of the cross want us to be content with just doing good deeds and not talking about Jesus. Traitors to the cross portray doctrinal uncertainty on the essentials as humility and confidence in Christ as anathema even to the "way of Jesus." It can all seem rather perplexing and draining and cause much consternation. The fight takes a lot out of us, and we can easily become weary. If contending is all duty and no delight, then we will eventually throw up our hands and say, "Can't we all just get along?"

But if contending is an active metaphor for living the Christian life intentionally, then it is not only hard work, it is *necessary* work. That's why Jude gives us a glimpse of its glory. If we see only the difficulty in the duty, we will miss the delight that comes with it, and there is delight.[162] Perhaps "delight" seems like a strange word to use in connection with everything we've talked about in this book. But it's what ultimately makes contending possible for the Christian. If you and I will be able to accept and continue this necessary work, we need delight in God and his promises as the fuel that powers our continued efforts.

Jude knows about the difficulty of contending and the divisions it may produce. He knows his readers will see the task set before them and want to weep. But he is a wise pastor, so he doesn't end his letter with a command or a quick wrist-slapping, "Now get back to work!" Instead, Jude ends his letter with magnificent praise to our Lord and Savior:

> Now to him who is able to keep you from stumbling and to present you blameless before the presence of his glory with great joy, to the only God, our Savior, through Jesus Christ our Lord, be glory, majesty, dominion, and authority, before all time and now and forever. Amen.[163]

Amen, indeed. Jude's closing words carry glorious assurance for the believer. Contend for the faith that was once and for all delivered to you because that faith is in a person whose joy you will one day enter. These words end Jude's letter because he wants his readers to receive hope and strength and delight as we contend.

God is able to keep us from stumbling and in the end present us to himself utterly blameless. Indeed, God will do this very thing for every one of his children. We are "called, beloved ... and kept for Jesus Christ,"[164] preserved for his purposes. No true believer can be snatched from his hand.[165] While Christians may sin, and sometimes in horrendous ways, God promises he will keep us from committing apostasy. We are Christ's, and *nothing* can draw us away forever: "neither death nor life, nor angels nor rulers, nor things present nor things to come, nor powers, nor height nor depth, nor anything else in all creation, will be able to separate us from the love of God in Christ Jesus our Lord."[166]

What assurance this gives us as we seek to contend on behalf of fellow believers! Because God preserves those who are his, we can have confidence that Christians swerving toward apostasy can be restored to the truth. We can know that no believer will ever run so fast or so far that God will not pull him back off the path of destruction. Not even the most appealing lie can capture the attention of a true Christian forever; those with ears to hear will never grow permanently deaf to the voice of Jesus.

We can hold fast to sound doctrine, contend for the truth, and persevere in the face of opposition with the full knowledge that our hope lies in God's love, not in our ability. *We keep ourselves in the love of God,*[167] growing strong doctrinally, persevering in prayer, and waiting for the Lord's return *through his strength*—and we are kept by the one who is able to keep us. So "work out your own salvation with fear and trembling," knowing "it is God who works in you, both to will and to work for his good pleasure."[168] And on that final day, when Christ returns to make all things new, when sin and death and lies are no more, we will stand before his presence with great joy, blameless and "without spot or blemish,"[169] presented and purified by him.

Do you see the delight that these truths bring to contending? Contend in our own strength, and all hope will soon be lost. On our best day and armed with our most convincing arguments, you and I are incapable of bringing a single soul to repentance. Not only that, left to ourselves we cannot even shine the light of grace on a single truth of the gospel in a way that will make any difference.

Every single incremental step in the progress of the gospel from the moment of the fall until now has come about by the grace, love, and mercy of God. So it is and will be in our every act of contending; it is God who will give the increase—not our strength, persistence, persuasiveness, charm, or cultural relevance. Despite our foolish words and wavering hearts, God delights to use us as his instruments. Let us delight in this as well! Our Father entrusts to us the ministry and message of reconciliation,[170] and he empowers and enables us to accomplish what he has called us to do. This ought to fill our hearts with unbridled joy, for our great God and Savior Jesus Christ intends to draw the wayward near to himself through our contending. What a privilege! What a *delight*.

May these truths fill our hearts with confidence, knowing that God is preserving those who are his. By his eternal power and unfailing promises we can contend with hearts full of joy as we glorify God through the display of his greatness in the gospel, standing firm for the truth once for all delivered to the saints.

This is our sacred duty. This is our great delight.

Endnotes

1. Jude 3
2. Two recent and helpful studies on this subject include *The Millennials: Connecting to America's Largest Generation* by Thom S. Rainer and Jess W. Rainer (Nashville, TN: B&H Publishing Group, 2011) and *You Lost Me: Why Young Christians Are Leaving Church … and Rethinking Faith* by David Kinnaman (Grand Rapids, MI: Baker Books, 2011).
3. Rainer, *The Millennials*, 18.
4. Ibid., 87–91.
5. Ibid., 153.
6. cf. Colossians 2:16
7. Ecclesiastes 1:14 (see also 2:11, 17, 26; 4:16; 6:9)
8. Rainer, *The Millennials*, 153.
9. cf. 1 Timothy 4:1
10. See Galatians 2:14 and 2 Corinthians 11:5, 13–15.
11. 1 John may have been written to combat a form of proto-Gnosticism that sought to subvert Christianity with religious mysticism.
12. Revelation 2:6, 15
13. For example, http://www.acts29network.org/article/put-the-advance-of-the-gospel-at-the-center-of-your-aspirations/
14. For two helpful analyses, see *Becoming Conversant with the Emerging Church* by D. A. Carson (Grand Rapids, MI: Zondervan, 2005) and *Listening to the Beliefs of Emerging Churches* edited by Robert Webber (Grand Rapids, MI: Zondervan, 2007).
15. The best-known practitioners of this methodology include Willow Creek Community Church in Barrington, IL, and Saddleback Community Church in Lake Forest, CA. In mentioning them, I am not criticizing Rick Warren or Bill Hybels or their motivations but am simply pointing to examples of what this looks like in practice.
16. Greg L. Hawkins and Cally Parkinson, *Reveal: Where Are You?* (Barrington IL: Willow Creek Resources, 2007), 35.
17. Ibid., 54.
18. Ibid., 55.
19. According to *Outreach Magazine*'s 2011 edition of the top 100

largest and fastest growing churches in America, the combined total attendance of these churches is 144,247. Please note: I have included Joel Osteen's church in this list because his methodology falls into the seeker movement, but it is worth noting that his theology does not gel with that of the seeker-sensitive movement as a whole. I am not equating Osteen's theology with that of the other men named in this paragraph.

20. This is an unhelpful term because it has not been defined well and is often confused with the Emergent Village, which is the revisionist group within the emerging church.

21. Doug Pagitt, "The Emerging Church and EmbodiedTheology," *Listening to the Beliefs of Emerging Churches*, 142.

22. Andy Crouch, "The Emergent Mystique," ChristianityToday.com, accessed March 12, 2012, http://www.christianitytoday.com/ct/2004/november/12.36.html.

23. Ibid.

24. Rob Bell, *Velvet Elvis* (Grand Rapids, MI: Zondervan, 2005), 114.

25. D. A. Carson wrote this about McLaren in his blazing critique of the "emerging church" movement: "I have to say, as kindly but as forcefully as I can, that to my mind, if words mean anything, [he has] largely abandoned the gospel" (*Becoming Conversant with the Emerging Church*, 186).

26. Crouch, "The Emergent Mystique."

27. Bell, *Velvet Elvis*, 27.

28. Luke 12:51

29. John 14:6

30. She was right: the Empire appears in "Battle for the Sunstar," the last episode of the series.

31. cf. Deuteronomy 29:29

32. Psalm 8:1

33. Genesis 2:7, 22

34. Psalm 139:13

35. Matthew 6:8

36. Genesis 1:1

37. Revelation 4:8; 21:6

38. Romans 1:25

39. See Genesis 1:1; John 3:16; Romans 8:29; Galatians 4:4; and Ephesians 1:3–5.

40. See John 1:1–3; Colossians 1:15–22; Hebrews 2:7, 9; Revelation 4:11; and 5:12 (cf. Daniel 7:13–14).
41. See John 14:16; Titus 3:3–5; Ephesians 4:30; and Romans 15:16.
42. Psalm 135:6 (cf. Isaiah 46:10)
43. Isaiah 40:13
44. Daniel 4:34–35
45. 1 John 4:8
46. Exodus 34:14
47. Nahum 1:2
48. Exodus 34:6
49. Isaiah 6:3 (cf. Revelation 4:8)
50. R. C. Sproul, *The Holiness of God* (Carol Stream, IL: Tyndale House, 1998), 40.
51. Richard Dawkins, *The God Delusion* (New York, NY: Mariner, 2008), 51.
52. Roger Olson, *Against Calvinism* (Grand Rapids, MI: Zondervan, 2011), 85.
53. 1 Corinthians 15:3–4
54. 1 John 4:10
55. John 5:39
56. Luke 24:25–27
57. Genesis 3:15
58. Isaiah 53:6
59. Jude 5a
60. For more on the authority of Scripture, see Sola Scriptura! *The Protestant Position on the Bible* edited by Don Kistler (Morgan, PA: Soli Deo Gloria, 1995).
61. Everyone holds something as sacred. Even those who insist nothing is sacred hold that belief to be sacred, or beyond question. You cannot get away from it.
62. Theological "liberals" may be the more familiar term, but many in that camp would prefer "progressive."
63. Both conservatives and liberals generally favor social progress for the common good. Significant differences arise, however, over what constitutes genuine social progress, how to achieve it, and how to anticipate or respond to the new expressions of sin that always accompany new freedoms.
64. James 3:8

65. Proverbs 10:19
66. Galatians 5:15
67. See Alexander Strauch, *If You Bite and Devour One Another* (Colorado Springs, CO: Lewis & Roth Publishers, 2011), 22.
68. This is not always easy, of course. If all secondary issues could be unambiguously derived from primary issues, there would far less division within Protestantism.
69. Jude 4a
70. Matthew 7:15
71. Acts 20:28–31
72. 2 Corinthians 11:13–15
73. Philippians 3:2
74. Colossians 2:18–19a
75. 1 Timothy 1:6–7
76. 2 Peter 2:1
77. 2 John 7
78. Galatians 1:8–9
79. Jude 12
80. Jude 11
81. Gen. esis 3:1
82. Rob Bell, *Love Wins: A Book About Heaven, Hell, and the Fate of Every Person Who Ever Lived* (New York, NY: HarperOne, 2011), 136–137.
83. Ibid. 107, 114–115.
84. Jude 15
85. D. A. Carson, *From the Resurrection to His Return*, (Ross-shire, Scotland: Christian Focus Publishers, 2010), Kindle edition.
86. Jude 20–21
87. Jude 21
88. 1 Timothy 4:16
89. Acts 2:42, Hebrews 10:24–25, and 1 John 4:7–8 are just a few of the dozens of passages illustrating this truth.
90. Jude 20–21
91. Ephesians 4:14
92. cf. Philippians 2:12
93. Jude 22–23
94. James 3:1
95. 1 Timothy 3:1–7

96. 1Timothy 3:4–5
97. Romans 1:15; 15:20
98. 2Timothy 4:2
99. Luke 4:43
100. Acts 10:42
101. Acts 6:4
102. See Luke 22:33, 54–62, and, to be fair, ask yourself: how many of us would have done better than Peter in that same circumstance?
103. 1 Peter 2:2
104. 2 Timothy 3:15
105. 2 Timothy 3:16
106. Hebrews 4:12
107. 1 Peter 2:3 (cf. Psalm 34:38; Hebrews 6:5)
108. Acts 20:18–27
109. R. C. Sproul, John, *St. Andrew's Expositional Commentary* (Wheaton, Il: Crossway, 2009), 406.
110. 1 Corinthians 5:6; Galatians 5:9
111. There are not always clear divisions between these categories. For example, sometimes in order to protect the majority of a congregation from error, a pastor must reprove and correct a minority of the members, even as for a season he feeds the overall church a teaching diet designed to strengthen it in a particular area.
112. For my purposes here, I have reversed the order of Mahaney's last two questions. Listen to the original presentation at http://www.thegospelcoalition.org/resources/a/pastoring_with_discernment_applying_the_gospel_to_the_hearts_of_those_.
113. Justin Holcomb of The Resurgence explains that Pelagianism says "Humans by nature have a clean slate, and it is only through voluntary sin that humans are made wicked. Potentially, then, one could live a sinless life and merit heaven" ("Pelagius: KnowYour Heretics,"TheResurgence.com, accessed March 21, 2012, http://theresurgence.com/2010/03/15/pelagius-know-your-heretics).
114. Lest you think I advocate ignoring the needs of the poor and oppressed, please see my book *Awaiting a Savior:The Gospel, the New Creation, and the End of Poverty* (Cruciform Press, 2011).

115. See Acts 20:28.
116. 1 Timothy 1:20; 2 Timothy 2:17–18
117. Revelation 2:6, 15–16
118. cf. Hebrews 13:18
119. Hebrews 13:17
120. Joshua Harris' Why Church Matters: Discovering Your Place in the Family of God (Colorado Springs, CO: Multnomah, 2011) addresses this subject well.
121. See Mark Dever's Nine Marks of a Healthy Church by Mark Dever (Wheaton, IL: Crossway, 2004), for example.
122. Ephesians 4:31
123. 1 Timothy 4:16
124. Jude 21
125. Philippians 2:12
126. Jude 20–21
127. Robert Gundry and Thomas R. Schreiner note these commands in their commentaries on Jude, and Schreiner observes the same in his study notes in *The ESV Study Bible*.
128. In saying this, I am not suggesting that everyone understands to the same degree but only to the capacity God has gifted them.
129. Carson, From the Resurrection to His Return (Kindle edition).
130. 2 Timothy 3:16
131. 2 Timothy 3:15
132. For a tremendously helpful book on this subject, see *Lit! A Christian Guide to Reading Books* by Tony Reinke (Wheaton, IL: Crossway Books, 2011).
133. Thomas R. Schreiner, *The New American Commentary*, Vol. 37: 1, 2 Peter, Jude (Nashville TN: Broadman & Holman Publishers, 2003), 483.
134. *A Simple Way to Pray: The Wisdom of Martin Luther on Prayer*, 5th ed., by Archie Parrish (Marietta, GA: Serve International, 2009), Kindle edition.
135. Schreiner, *The New American Commentary*, Vol. 37: 1, 2, Peter, Jude, 483.
136. Luke 22:40
137. Acts 1:14
138. Acts 3:1

139. Acts 6:4
140. Acts 12:5
141. James 5:14–16
142. Proverbs 12:18
143. Proverbs 18:21
144. See John 13:35
145. Titus 2:13
146. Philippians 3:20–21
147. Romans 8:23
148. Galatians 5:5
149. Robert H. Gundry, *Commentary on First and Second Peter, Jude* (Grand Rapids, MI: Baker Academic, 2010), Kindle edition.
150. Ephesians 6:12
151. cf. 2 Peter 1:3–8
152. 1 Timothy 6:4
153. Titus 3:1–2
154. Titus 3:10–11
155. Philippians 2:3–4
156. Revelation 2:2–3
157. Revelation 2:4–5
158. Ephesians 1:15
159. Sam Storms, *To the One Who Conquers: 50 Daily Meditations on the Seven Letters of Revelation 2–3* (Wheaton IL: Crossway, 2008), 50 (Kindle edition).
160. Ibid.
161. cf. Luke 14:26
162. See John Piper for more on this juxtaposition of duty and delight.
163. Jude 24–25
164. Jude 1
165. John 10:28–29
166. Romans 8:37–39
167. Jude 21
168. Philippians 2:12–13
169. 2 Peter 3:14
170. 2 Corinthians 5:18–19

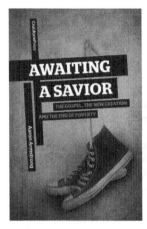

Awaiting a Savior
The Gospel, the New Creation and the End of Poverty

by Aaron Armstrong

Christians are called to serve the poor generously, joyfully, by grace, to the glory of God.

But eliminating poverty is a misguided and dangerous goal.

Poverty is rooted in the fall of man, and there is only one Savior.

"Challenging our own idolatry, our own motivations, and our own actions, *Awaiting a Savior* reorients our mercy ministry around the gospel, seeking to show how a life of love is the overflow of a grace-filled heart."

Trevin Wax, author, editor at Lifeway Christian Resources

"Aaron Armstrong is rightly pessimistic about humanistic solutions, brightly optimistic about God's ultimate solution, and practically realistic about the best and most the Church can do in this present age."

Dr. David P. Murray, Puritan Reformed Theological Seminary

"*Awaiting a Savior* gets at the real but often overlooked cause of poverty. It is a solid theological treatment of what poverty really stems from and how to see it within a biblical framework."

Pastor Dave Kraft, Mars Hill Church, Orange County, author

"Finally, a book that tackles the subject of poverty in a biblical, balanced, thought-provoking, and convicting manner! Walks the fine line of calling for a biblical solution to poverty without causing the reader to feel overly burdened with unnecessary, unbiblical guilt. Aaron also shows how biblical generosity is ultimately rooted in the generosity of God himself."

Stephen Altrogge, pastor, author, TheBlazingCenter.com

The Two Fears
Tremble Before God Alone

by Chris Poblete

**You can fear God...
or everything else.**

**Only one fear brings life and hope,
wisdom and joy.**

Fear wisely.

"We are too scared. And we aren't scared enough. Reading this book
will prompt you to seek in your own life the biblical tension between
'fear not' and 'fear God.'"
>*Russell D. Moore, Dean, Southern Baptist Theological Seminary*

"An importantly counter-cultural book, moving us beyond a
homeboy God we could fist-bump to a holy God we can worship.
The Two Fears helps us recover a biblical fear of God and all the awe,
repentance, and freedom from self-centered fears that go with it. An
awesome resource!"
>*Dr. Thaddeus Williams, professor, Biola University*

"In this practical and very readable book, Chris Poblete shows how
both the absence of true fear and the presence of 'unholy [false] fear'
stem from an absence of a knowledge of the awesome God of the
Bible, and that, in meeting him, we discover the real dimensions of
creational existence and the wonderful benefits of living in fear and
deep respect before him, freed from the '[false] fear of men.'"
>*Peter Jones, Ph.D., TruthXchange; Scholar-in-Residence and
Adjunct Professor, Westminster Seminary in California*

"I commend this book to you: it will fuel your worship and empower
your discipleship."
>*Gabe Tribbett, Christ's Covenant Church, Winona Lake, IA*

Killing Calvinism
How to Destroy a Perfectly Good Theology from the Inside

by Greg Dutcher

A resurgence of Calvinism is changing lives, transforming churches, and spreading the gospel. Will it continue or will we destroy it?

That depends on how we live the message.

"Brilliant corrective work and I couldn't be more glad he wrote it."
Matt Chandler, The Village Church; President, Acts 29

"When this kind of critique and warning come from within a movement, it is a sign of health."
John Piper, Desiring God

"This book blew me away! Greg Dutcher skillfully diagnoses how I kill the very truth I love by my hypocrisy, pride, anger, and judgmental attitude. This book will serve a young generation of Calvinists. But the older generation had better heed it, too. There's medicine here for all our hearts."
Thabiti Anyabwile, author; Senior Pastor, First Baptist Church, Grand Cayman; Council Member, The Gospel Coalition

""Dutcher's wisdom will go a long way in bringing spiritual health to the young, restless, and reformed."
Sam Storms, Bridgeway Church, Oklahoma City

"An absolute must-read for every YRR–and older Calvinists too! With wit, compassion, and candor, Greg Dutcher exposes how sin taints our theological convictions... he shows us Calvinism done right to the glory of God."
Lydia Brownback, author and speaker

CPSIA information can be obtained at www.ICGtesting.com
Printed in the USA
BVOW08s2225110714

358822BV00005B/10/P